JUSTUS LIPSIUS

———————

ON CONSTANCY

John Sellars is a Research Fellow at Wolfson College, Oxford and Assistant Editor for the 'Ancient Commentators on Aristotle' project at King's College London. He is author of *The Art of Living: The Stoics on the Nature and Function of Philosophy* (2003) and *Stoicism* (2006).

MORIBVS ANTIQVIS   Ætat. 40. An° 1587

IVSTVS LIPSIVS
Iuste, decus Patriæ, Latij sermonis ocelle,
Vt Sophiâ præstas, sic pietate nites.

Crispin de Pas fecit   Balth. Caimox exc.

Engraving of Justus Lipsius (from the editor's collection)

JUSTUS LIPSIUS

ON CONSTANCY

De Constantia translated by
Sir John Stradling (1595)

edited with an introduction, notes and bibliography
by John Sellars

BRISTOL
PHOENIX
PRESS

Cover image: from an engraving belonging to the editor.

First published in 2006 by
Bristol Phoenix Press
an imprint of The Exeter Press
Reed Hall, Streatham Drive,
Exeter, Devon EX4 4QR
UK
www.exeterpress.co.uk

British Library Cataloguing in Publication Data
A catalogue record for this book is available
from the British Library.

ISBN 10: 1 904675 15 8
ISBN 13: 978 1 904675 15 0

Printed and bound by CPI Group (UK) Ltd, Croydon, CR0 4YY

TABLE OF CONTENTS

ABBREVIATIONS

In general, references containing a full stop (e.g. 2.30) refer to book and chapter or chapter and section, while those containing a comma (e.g. 15,4) refer to a volume and page or a page and line.

Works by Lipsius

Const.	*De Constantia Libri Duo* (1584); repr. in *Opera* 4,511-612
Man.	*Manuductio ad Stoicam Philosophiam* (1604); repr. in *Opera* 4,613-821
Opera	*Opera Omnia*, 4 vols (1675; repr. Hildesheim: Georg Olms, 2003)
Phys.	*Physiologia Stoicorum* (1604); repr. in *Opera* 4,823-1007
Pol.	*Politicorum sive Civilis Doctrinae Libri Sex* (1589); repr. in *Opera* 4,1-195

'Kirk', 'Neumann', and 'Du Bois' refer to the editions of *De Constantia* by those editors, the details of which may be found on pp. 21-22 below.

Other Abbreviations

CAF	*Comicorum Atticorum Fragmenta*, ed. T. Kock (Leipzig: Teubner, 1880-88)
CCSL	*Corpus Christianorm, Series Latina* (Turnhout: Brepols)
DK	H. Diels & W. Kranz, *Die Fragmente der Vorsokratiker*, 3 vols (Zürich & Berlin: Weidmann, 1964)
DPhA	*Dictionnaire des Philosophes Antiques*, ed. R. Goulet, 4 vols to date (Paris: CNRS, 1994-)
LCL	Loeb Classical Library (Cambridge, MA: Harvard University Press)
PG	*Patrologiae Graeca*, ed. J.-P. Migne, 162 vols (Paris, 1857-66)

PL   *Patrologiae Latina*, ed. J.-P. Migne, 221 vols (Paris, 1844-55)
SSR   *Socratis et Socraticorum Reliquiae*, ed. G. Giannantoni, 4 vols
          (Naples: Bibliopolis, 1990)
SVF   *Stoicorum Veterum Fragmenta*, ed. H. von Arnim, 4 vols
          (Leipzig: Teubner, 1903-24)

PREFACE

This volume contains a lightly revised edition of Sir John Stradling's translation of Justus Lipsius' *De Constantia*, first published in 1595, and reprinted with editorial material by Rudolf Kirk in 1939. Kirk's edition, now long out of print, retains the original sixteenth century spellings and other typographical conventions. By contrast, in this edition I have modernised Stradling's spelling and punctuation throughout and often reworded phrases. I have not hesitated, for instance, to change 'be thou not' to 'do not be', 'think ye' to 'do you think' and 'quoth he' to 'he said'. On occasions I have consulted the Latin text in order to determine how best to replace an archaic term or form of words. However, I have not gone through and corrected Stradling's translation line by line against the Latin. Despite my modernisations, the translation remains his.

I have contributed the introduction, notes, an analysis of the contents of the text and a bibliographical guide to Lipsius' philosophical works. In many cases my notes draw upon those in previous editions by Kirk and Neumann (although some of their references have proved to be incorrect). The vast majority of ancient works mentioned in the notes are referred to by their standard Latin titles. All Greek is transliterated. In general I have consulted the readily available Loeb Classical Library editions of ancient authors, where they exist. For all other authors I supply details of the editions consulted in the Index of Passages. I have not attempted to collate the divergences between Lipsius' versions of his quotations and the versions in modern editions; the difference is sometimes considerable. In some instances I have not been able to locate Lipsius' source; and neither have Neumann or Kirk. I have not thought it necessary to add uninformative notes simply stating 'source unknown' in all of these places.

Although I have consulted a copy of Stradling's 1595 edition in the British Library, I have relied upon Kirk's edition for Stradling's text. I have consulted a number of different editions of Lipsius' Latin text but I have, in general, relied upon (what is to the best of my knowledge) the most recent edition by Neumann. Capitalisation of certain terms is not always consistent; in general it reflects the texts of both Lipsius and Stradling. Regarding Stradling's translation, I have found it rarely misleading, although it does not always capture Lipsius' style. Readers should note that Stradling renders *fatum* – a key term – as both 'fate' and 'destiny', sometimes as 'fate or destiny' or 'fatal destiny'.

INTRODUCTION

Philosophie in generall is profitable unto a Christian man, if it be well and rightly used: but no kinde of philosophie is more profitable and neerer approaching unto Christianitie than the philosophie of the Stoicks.[1]

Background

The claim – here in the words of Thomas James – that the ancient philosophy of Stoicism can be profitably reconciled with Christianity has a long and varied history. Stoicism was one of the great Hellenistic schools of philosophy and it flourished in antiquity for at least 400 years.[2] Founded by Zeno of Citium around 300 BC, the school developed under Cleanthes, Chrysippus, Panaetius, and Posidonius. In the first century BC it appealed to high-ranking Romans including Cicero and Cato. In the first two centuries AD it reached its height of popularity under the influence of Seneca, Musonius Rufus, and Epictetus. In the second century AD it found perhaps its most famous exponent in the Roman emperor Marcus Aurelius. However, after the second century Stoicism was soon eclipsed in popularity by Neoplatonism.

The earliest attempts to reconcile Stoicism with Christianity can be seen in the works of a number of the Latin Church Fathers.[3] St. Augustine showed sympathy towards the Stoic doctrine of *apatheia*, while Tertullian was drawn towards Stoic materialism. However, none of these Christian authors wholly endorsed the Stoic philosophical system. Indeed, they often differed with regard to which parts of Stoic philosophy they thought could be reconciled with orthodox Christian teaching.

Stoicism continued to exert influence throughout the Christian Middle Ages.[4] Adaptations of Epictetus' *Enchiridion* made for use in monasteries (references to 'Socrates' being altered to 'St. Paul'),

1

highlight the perceived affinity between the Christian and the Stoic way of life.[5] Seneca's *Epistulae* circulated and appear to have been read by many.[6] Stoic ethical ideas can be seen in the moral works of Peter Abelard, especially in the *Dialogus inter Philosophum, Iudaeum et Christianum*.[7]

In each of these instances Stoic moral ideas were taken out of the broader context of the Stoic philosophical system and placed within a Christian context. It is sometimes claimed that this practice simply reflected the predominance of moral themes within the available sources, namely the Latin works of Seneca and Cicero. However, at least some knowledge of Stoic physics was readily accessible in works such as Cicero's *De Natura Deorum, De Divinatione*, and *De Fato*. The existence of a forged correspondence between Seneca and St. Paul, accepted as genuine by St. Augustine and St. Jerome, may well have contributed to the thought that it was possible to combine Stoic ethics with Christian teaching.

In the fourteenth century Stoicism attracted the attention of Petrarch, who produced a substantial ethical work entitled *De Remediis Utriusque Fortunae* inspired by Seneca and drawing upon an account of the Stoic theory of the passions made by Cicero.[8] With new Humanist translations of Epictetus' *Enchiridion* by Perotti and Politian in the fifteenth century, interest in Stoicism continued to develop.[9]

However, the most important attempt to reconcile Stoicism with Christianity is to be found in Justus Lipsius' *De Constantia*, first published in 1584. Its importance is due in part to its subsequent influence. Its impact led to the philosophical movement that has come to be known as 'Neostoicism'.[10] Lipsius' *De Constantia* outlines the way in which a Christian may, in times of trouble, draw upon a Stoic-inspired ethic of constancy (*constantia*) to help him to endure the evils of the world. As Lipsius makes clear in a prefatory letter to the work, he was the first to 'have attempted the opening and clearing of this way of wisdom [i.e. Stoicism], so long recluded and overgrown with thorns'.[11] Yet in order to do this, Lipsius had to present the pagan philosophy in a form that could be reconciled with Christianity. Thus he makes clear in the same letter that it is only in conjunction with holy scriptures (*cum divinis litteris conjuncta*) that this ancient way of wisdom (*Sapientiae viam*) can lead to tranquillity and peace (*ad Tranquillitatem et Quietem*).[12]

Lipsius' Life

Justus Lipsius (the Latinised version of Joest Lips) was born in Overyssche, a village near Brussels and Louvain, in 1547.[13] He studied first with the Jesuits in Cologne and later at the Catholic University of Louvain. After completing his education he visited Rome, in his new position as secretary to Cardinal Granvelle, staying for two years in order to study the ancient monuments and explore the unsurpassed libraries of classical literature. In 1572 Lipsius' property in Belgium was taken by Spanish troops during the civil war while he was away on a trip to Vienna – a trip that would later be used as the backdrop for the dialogue in *De Constantia* over a decade later. Deprived of his property, Lipsius applied for a position at the Lutheran University of Jena. This was the first of a number of institutional moves that required him to change his publicly professed faith. His new colleagues at Jena remained sceptical of this radical transformation and after only two years Lipsius was eventually forced to leave Jena in favour of Cologne, where he prepared notes on Tacitus that he used in his critical edition of 1574.

In 1576 Lispius returned to Catholic Louvain. However, after his property was looted by soldiers a second time he fled again in 1579, this time to the Calvinist University of Leiden. He remained there for thirteen years and it is to this period that his two most famous books – *De Constantia Libri Duo* (1584) and *Politicorum sive Civilis Doctrinae Libri Sex* (1589) – belong. However, Lipsius was by upbringing a Catholic and eventually he sought to return to Louvain, via a brief period in Liège. In 1592 Lipsius accepted the Chair of Latin History and Literature at Louvain and to this final period belong his editorial work on Seneca and his two detailed studies of Stoicism, the *Manuductio ad Stoicam Philosophiam* and *Physiologia Stoicorum*. These two studies were published first in 1604 and the edition of Seneca in 1605. He died in Louvain in 1606.

Among Lipsius' friends was his publisher, the famous printer Christopher Plantin, with whom he often stayed in Antwerp.[14] Among his pupils was Philip Rubens, brother of the painter Peter Paul Rubens who portrayed Lipsius after his death in 'The Four Philosophers' (*c.* 1611, now in the Pitti Palace, Florence).[15] Among his admirers was Michel de Montaigne, who described him as one of the most learned men then alive.[16]

Lipsius' Works

Lipsius was a prolific author,[17] publishing his first work *Variarum Lectionum Libri IV* – a collection of philological comments and conjectures – in 1569, while in his twenties.[18] His reputation today is primarily as a Latin philologist and stands upon his critical editions of Tacitus and Seneca. He also produced a number of philological studies and a large correspondence, much of which he published.[19] His principal philosophical works are *De Constantia Libri Duo* and *Politicorum sive Civilis Doctrinae Libri Sex* (*Politica* for short). The former, dealing with ethical themes, reflects his interest in Seneca; the latter, a treatise on politics, reflects his interest in Tacitus.

a) *Politica*

In his *Politica* Lipsius drew upon a wide range of classical sources, with a particular emphasis upon Tacitus, and the work has been characterised, not unfairly, as not much more than a compendium of quotations.[20] In it he argued that no State should permit more than one religion within its borders and that all dissent should be punished without mercy. Experience had taught him that civil conflict enflamed by religious intolerance was far more dangerous and destructive than despotism.

The treatise is concerned with the creation of civil life, defined as 'that which we lead in the society of men, one with another, to mutual commodity and profit, and common use of all'.[21] Such a life has two necessary conditions, virtue (*virtus*) and prudence (*prudentia*). Book One is devoted to an analysis of these two conditions: virtue requires piety and goodness; prudence is dependent upon use and memory. Book Two opens by arguing that government is necessary for civil life and that the best form of government is a Principality. Civil concord requires all to submit to the will of one. 'Principality' (*principatus*) is defined as 'rule by one for the good of all'.[22] For the Prince to achieve this he himself must have both virtue and prudence. The remainder of Book Two is devoted to princely virtues, the most important being justice and clemency. Book Three moves on to consider princely prudence, and this remains the theme for the rest of the work. There are two types of prudence, one's own and the advice of others. Book Three focuses upon prudent advisors in the form of counsellors and ministers. Book Four is concerned with a Prince's own prudence, which must be carefully developed in the light of experience. This itself may be divided into civil and military prudence. The rest of Book Four outlines two types of civil prudence, that concerned with matters divine and that concerned with matters human. Military Prudence is the subject of Books Five and Six. Book Five deals with external military prudence (war with foreign powers), while Book Six deals with internal military prudence (civil war).

The central theme of the work is clear from the outset. Lipsius – pre-empting Hobbes – places order and peace far above civil liberties and personal freedom. Individual political rights are little consolation if one is surrounded by violent anarchy. The first task for politics is to secure peace for all and this can only be done if power is concentrated in one individual. It can also only be achieved if only one religion is allowed in any particular State. If one has concerns about such a concentration of power, the proper way to reduce them is to educate the holder of power, to develop his virtue and prudence, and to remind him that he holds power in order to secure peace, not to create terror. If a Prince forgets this last point and turns into a tyrant, there may be grounds to challenge his position. Lipsius emphasises, however, that there is nothing more miserable than civil war, which should be avoided at all costs.

b) *De Constantia*

Lipsius' principal philosophical work is *De Constantia Libri Duo*, published in 1584 (its title echoes that of Seneca's dialogue *De Constantia Sapientis*). This work proved to be immensely popular and went through numerous editions,[23] it was translated into English four times between 1595 and 1670,[24] and it was for this work that Lipsius became famous in the succeeding centuries, inspiring the intellectual movement that has come to be known as Neostoicism. It was conceived as an attempt to revive Stoicism as a living philosophy (as it had been in antiquity) and, in particular, as a practical antidote to public evils.

De Constantia takes the form of a dialogue between Lipsius and his friend Langius (Charles de Langhe, Canon of Liège).[25] This no doubt fictional conversation is set within the context of a visit to Langius by Lipsius during the course of a trip to Vienna – the one that Lipsius had actually undertaken in 1572. While some distance from his troubled homeland, the dialogue's character Lipsius reflects upon the nature of public evils (*mala publica*) and is guided by the older and wiser Langius into whose mouth the positive content of the dialogue is placed.

Book One opens (chs 1-3) by explaining that Lipsius' trip was an attempt to escape the evils of civil war then raging in the Low Countries. Langius begins this discussion with the traditional Stoic claim that it would be a mistake to think that it is ever possible to run away from such evils for at bottom they are the product of one's own opinions.[26] He cites a Socratic anecdote preserved by Seneca in which when a man asked why travel did him no good, Socrates responded by saying that it was because he always took himself with him.[27] As Langius puts it, the mind must be changed, not the place.[28]

After these preliminary remarks the central concept of *constantia* is introduced (ch. 4). It is defined as 'a right and immovable strength of the mind, neither elated nor depressed by external or chance events'.[29] The mother of *constantia* is *patientia* or patience, defined as 'a voluntary endurance without complaint of all things that can happen to or in a man'.[30] After these definitions, a sharp distinction is drawn (chs 5-6) between reason (*ratio*) and opinion (*opinio*). Opinion, says Langius, is unsure of itself and so leads in inconstancy, whereas reason is secure and so forms the foundation for constancy. Cultivating reason is thus the way by which one can reach the goal of constancy, defined as freedom from 'the servile yoke of fortune and affections'.[31] After an examination of a number of the affections that stand as the enemies of constancy (chs 7-12) – the chief being desire (*cupiditas*), joy (*gaudium*), fear (*metus*), and sorrow (*dolor*) – Langius moves on to outline the content of the remainder of the work by introducing four main arguments concerned with the nature of public evils (*mala publica*).[32] The first two arguments – that public evils are imposed by God and that they are the product of necessity – occupy the

remainder of Book One (chs 13-22). The second two arguments
– that they are in reality profitable for us and that they are neither
grievous nor unusual – occupy the bulk of Book Two (chs 6-26).[33]

The first argument claims that all public evils form part of
God's plan. In a passage reminiscent of the Stoic dog-cart analogy,
it is argued that if one does not follow God's will freely, one will
nevertheless be drawn along forcibly.[34] Our only option is, following
the advice of Seneca, to endure the human lot (*ferre mortalia*) and to
obey God (*deo parere*).[35]

The second argument focuses on the continual transformation
of the physical world according to the laws of causality. If even the
stars are subject to creation and destruction then it is only natural
that cities will rise and fall, for 'all things run into this fatal whirlpool
of ebbing and flowing'.[36] However, Langius is careful to distance
himself from heretical Stoic materialist determinism and he outlines
four points on which the Stoic doctrine must be modified. These
are the claims that God is submitted to fate, that there is a natural
order of causes (and thus no miracles), that there is no contingency,
and that there is no free will.[37] Here we meet the limits of Lipsius'
Stoicism and the nature of the compromise between Stoicism and
Christianity in his Neostoicism.[38] Book One concludes by exhorting
the reader to follow God (*deum sequi*) and to obey necessity (*necessitate
obsequi*).[39]

After a brief interlude emphasising that the task at hand is philosophical rather than philological, the bulk of Book Two contains
the remaining two arguments concerning public evils. The third
argument, in Book Two, is merely a variation upon traditional
Christian responses to the problem of evil. Langius suggests that
public evils sent by God must in some sense be profitable for us,
suggesting that for the good (*bonos*) they constitute exercise (*exercendi*),
for the weak-willed (*lapsos*) correction (*castigandi*), and for the bad
(*improbos*) punishment (*puniendi*).[40] If these instances of God's 'justice'
appear misguided to us, we are simply told that it is not our place to
judge what God sees fit to impose on humankind. Instead we should
'willingly and indifferently bear these great public miseries' in the
knowledge that they issue from God's just will.[41]

The fourth and final argument suggests that the public evils
then suffered by the Low Countries are neither particularly grievous

nor uncommon. To illustrate this Langius draws upon numerous ancient examples of wars, plagues, and acts of cruelty from Jewish, Greek, and Roman history, listing death toll after death toll from historic battles, in order to put present-day troubles into context.[42] The conflict from which Lipsius has fled is neither excessively brutal nor particularly unusual, Langius suggests. What would be genuinely unusual would be an individual person insulated and exempted from the common law of birth and death, creation and destruction.[43] It is the human lot to suffer; the task is to decide how one faces that suffering. One can do so with sorrow (*dolor*) or with constancy (*constantia*). Sorrow is an affection that is the product of insecure opinions. Constancy, on the other hand, is a form of wisdom, the product of reason, and the only source of comfort and courage amid the sea of sorrows.[44]

The central theme of *De Constantia* – that public evils are the product of the mind that must be treated rather than fled – contrasts sharply with Lipsius' own earlier behaviour when faced with the religious wars then raging. Perhaps experience had taught him that, no matter how many geographical moves he made, he would not be able to escape the evils surrounding him until he examined himself. Only wisdom and constancy – the products of philosophical reflection – can bring true peace of mind.

c) *Later Stoic Works*

De Constantia was not Lipsius' only work devoted to Stoicism. He also produced two studies of Stoic philosophy during the course of the preparation of his 1605 edition of Seneca; the *Manuductio ad Stoicam Philosophiam* and the *Physiologia Stoicorum*, both published in 1604.[45] These two works offer an interpretation of every aspect of Stoic philosophy and draw together under subject headings large numbers of quotations and doxographical reports preserved in a wide range of ancient authors. These two works may be seen as the precursors to the, now standard, edition of the fragments of the early Stoics compiled by Hans von Arnim (*SVF*).

These later studies of Stoicism – based upon a more systematic survey of the surviving sources – are marked by two features which distinguish them from *De Constantia*. The first is a more developed awareness of the systematic inter-relation between ethics and physics in Stoic philosophy; the second is a revised and more positive attitude towards the Stoic theory of determinism. In *Phys.* 1.12, for instance, Lipsius demonstrates a more thorough understanding of the Stoic theory of fate, and on the basis of this he suggests that it can in fact be reconciled with Christian doctrine without modification. In order to do this, he draws upon St. Augustine's discussion of Stoic definitions of fate in *De Civitate Dei* 5.8 where it is argued that fate does not impinge upon the power of God but rather is the expression of the will of God.[46]

While *De Constantia* was a popular and highly readable dialogue, these later studies were primarily works of classical scholarship. They were conceived as supplementary volumes designed to complement Lipsius' final great work, his 1605 critical edition of the philosophical works of Seneca. This handsome folio edition included all of Seneca's prose works, detailed summaries for each, commentary, and a biography of the great Roman Stoic.[47] In this final publication, Lipsius' admiration of Stoic philosophy and his talents as a classical philologist are united so as to form a highly appropriate culmination to his intellectual career.

Later Impact: Neostoicism

The immediate impact of Lipsius' *De Constantia* can be measured by the number of times the text was reissued and how quickly it was translated into the major European languages.[48] Its lasting impact can be seen in the works of a whole host of authors who drew upon its central tenets and emulated its attempt to reconcile Stoicism with Christianity.[49] The collective efforts of Lipsius and his followers have come to be known as Neostoicsm,[50] although it was never an organised intellectual movement, and so consequently modern scholars do not always agree upon a fixed list of Neostoics. When used in its most restricted sense, the term is reserved only for Justus Lipsius and Guillaume Du Vair. In its widest sense, it is applied to almost any sixteenth or seventeenth century author whose works display the influence of Stoic ideas.

Guillaume Du Vair (1556-1621), a French statesman, onetime clerk councillor to the Paris parliament, and later Bishop of Lisieux, was an admirer of Lipsius. He wrote his own treatise *De la Constance* in 1594.[51] While Lipsius had been influenced by Seneca, Du Vair drew his inspiration from Epictetus. He translated the latter's *Enchiridion* into French (*c.* 1586) and characterised his own treatise, the *Philosophie morale des Stoïques*, as merely a reconstructed version of the *Enchiridion*, rewritten and reorganised in order to make its doctrines more accessible to the public.[52]

In *Philosophie morale des Stoïques* Du Vair treads a very careful path indeed in his attempt to combine Christianity with his admiration for Epictetus. He suggests that, although it would be improper for anyone to prefer the profane and puddle water of the pagan philosophers to the clear and sacred fountain of God's word, nevertheless the Stoics must be acknowledged as the greatest reproach to Christianity, insofar as they managed to live the noblest and most virtuous lives without the true light of the Christian God to guide them.

Following Epictetus, Du Vair argues that one should not concern oneself with external possessions. In particular, he suggests that the desire for great wealth is often the cause of great unhappiness. If one can free oneself from the passions of hope, despair, fear, and anger, then it will become possible to confront the trials and misfortunes of life without any great concern. Of particular interest, however, is the way in which Du Vair synthesises the Stoic doctrine of *apatheia* with his Christian belief. For him, complete mastery of one's passions, achieved via the application of Stoic principles, does not contradict Christian teaching but rather can form the basis for a truly Christian way of life. Only one who has overcome the passions of fear and anger can, for instance, practise true Christian forgiveness towards one's enemies.

Pierre Charron (1541-1603), a French churchman and associate of Michel de Montaigne, has been characterised as a figure in the Pyrrhonist revival and thus is arguably as much a Neosceptic as a Neostoic.[53] His principal philosophical work *De la sagesse*, first published in 1601,[54] focuses upon the image of the Stoic ethical ideal – the wise man or sage (*sophos*) – and the task of progressing towards that ideal. It is not just a treatise on ethics but primarily a guide to the life of wisdom, a guide to 'making progress' (*prokopê*), following the form of Epictetus' *Enchiridion*.

In the first book of *De la sagesse* Charron focuses upon self-knowledge and self-examination; in the second book he focuses upon behaviour; in the third he outlines the traditional virtues of prudence, justice, fortitude, and temperance. The work was incredibly popular in its day, having appeared in thirty-six editions by 1672. Yet it is less an original treatise and more a compendium of existing material, drawing upon a variety of other authors both ancient and modern. In particular, Charron has often been accused of plagiarising from Montaigne on a grand scale. He also openly acknowledges his debt to Neostoicism. In one of his prefatory notes, he writes that, 'this subject has indeed had a great right done to it by Lipsius already, who wrote an excellent treatise, in a method peculiar to himself, but the substance of it you will find all transplanted here'.[55] Charron also acknowledges his debt to Du Vair, 'to whom I have been much beholding, and from whom I have borrowed a great deal of what I shall say upon this subject of the passions'.[56]

Francisco de Quevedo (1580-1645), who held positions at the royal court of Spain,[57] produced a Spanish translation of Epictetus and a short work entitled *Doctrina Estoica*, which were published together in 1635.[58] The latter work was the second Neostoic text to appear in Spanish, pre-dated only by a translation of Lipsius' *De Constantia*, which appeared in 1616.[59] Here, and throughout his works, Quevedo draws upon Seneca and Epictetus, quoting both of these Stoic authorities often, as well as relying heavily upon Lipsius' *Manuductio*.[60]

In the *Doctrina Estoica* Quevedo attempted to connect Stoic thought with the Bible. Noting that the founder of Stoicism, Zeno, was of Semitic origin, Quevedo claimed that the biblical account of Job's heroic endurance in the face of adversity was the inspiration behind Stoic philosophy. The doctrines of Epictetus are thus, he suggests, simply formal ethical principles extrapolated from the actions of Job. Yet despite this bold, if untenable, vindication of Stoicism, Quevedo remains wary of calling himself a Stoic: he concludes his essay saying 'I would not myself boast of being a Stoic, but I hold them in high esteem'.[61]

Although it would probably be incorrect to call the famous French essayist Michel de Montaigne (1533-92) a 'Neostoic', Neo-stoic tendencies can be discerned in his work.[62] He certainly admired

Justus Lipsius, describing him as one of the most learned men then alive.[63] His general admiration of Seneca can be seen in *Essai* 2.10, *On Books*, and is repeated in *Essai* 2.32, *In Defence of Seneca and Plutarch*. In *Essai* 1.33 he draws attention to a parallel between Seneca and early Christians with regard to their attitudes towards death, while *Essai* 1.14 is devoted to an explication of a saying by Epictetus (that people are upset not by things, but by their judgements about things). However, Montaigne's mature view doubted the rational abilities of man and certainly would not have endorsed the ambitious Stoic ideal of the superhuman sage (*sophos*). Nevertheless he remained drawn to it, writing that, 'if a man cannot attain to that noble Stoic impassibility, let him hide in the lap of this peasant insensitivity of mine. What Stoics did from virtue I teach myself to do from temperament'.[64] Montaigne's engagement with Stoicism thus forms an important part of the revival of interest in Stoic philosophy associated with Neostoicism and it was no doubt inspired in part by Lipsius.

Stoicism after Neostoicism

Neostoicism proved influential in the last decades of the sixteenth century and the first decades of the seventeenth century. Later in the seventeenth century a number of authors began to criticise Stoicism and its modern interpreters. Some authors – such as Pascal and Malebranche – attacked Stoicism for its arrogant pride;[65] others – such as Bramhall and Cudworth – attacked it for its materialism and its determinism.[66] In each case an increasing number of authors began to doubt that Stoicism could be smoothly reconciled with Christianity.

In the last decades of the seventeenth century Spinoza's philosophy appeared on the intellectual scene and soon became the centre of controversy.[67] Spinozism was seen as a dangerous philosophy of determinism that denied miracles and identified God with material nature. Before long contemporaries began to note similarities between Spinozism and Stoicism;[68] Spinoza was presented as a latter day Stoic, and the Stoics were seen as the Spinozists of their day.[69] Before long both philosophies were denounced as dangerous forms of atheism.[70] By 1765 it was possible for Diderot to proclaim in the

Encyclopédie that 'Il n'est pas difficile de conclure de ces principes, que les stoïciens étoient matérialistes, fatalists, & à proprement parler athées'.[71]

This dramatic shift in the reception of Stoicism would presumably have horrified Lipsius. It reflected a change in the way in which Stoic sources were approached. For Lipsius and Du Vair, Stoicism was to be found in the texts of Seneca and Epictetus, and there they found a noble moral philosophy that prefigured aspects of Christian teaching, so they argued. By the end of the seventeenth century, however, critics attempted to reconstruct early Stoicism as a philosophical system from the surviving fragments, trying to determine its central tenets, and to capture its essence.[72] And when they did this, what they found was a precursor of Spinozism that – like its modern counterpart – identified God with nature, proposed universal determinism, and claimed that emotions are the product of human judgements. Ironically, the groundwork necessary for this new method of interpretation was laid by Lipsius himself when he made the first systematic, if incomplete, collections of Stoic fragments in the *Manuductio* and *Physiologia*.

NOTES TO INTRODUCTION

1. Thomas James (first librarian of the Bodleian in Oxford), from his dedicatory epistle that prefaces his English translation of Guillaume Du Vair's *The Moral Philosophie of the Stoicks*, published in 1598 (p. 45 in Kirk's edition).
2. For general literature introducing Stoicism see Sandbach (1975), Inwood (2003), and now Sellars (2006).
3. See Spanneut (1957) and (1973), 138-78; Colish (1985), vol. 2.
4. See the discussions in Verbeke (1983), Lapidge (1988), and Ebbesen (2004).
5. For the adapted texts see Boter (1999).
6. For Seneca's later influence see Reynolds (1965) and Ross (1974).
7. Text and translation in Marenbon and Orlandi (2001).
8. Translated in Rawski (1991); discussion in Panizza (1991).
9. See Oliver (1954) and Kraye (1997b). For wider discussions of Stoicism in the Renaissance see Bouwsma (1975) and Kraye (2004).
10. The term 'Neostoicism' appears to have been coined by Jean Calvin. In his *Institutio Religionis Christianae* of 1536, Calvin made reference to 'new Stoics' (*novi Stoici*) who attempted to revive the ideal of impassivity (*apatheia*) instead of embracing the properly Christian virtue of heroically enduring suffering sent by God (*Institutio* 3.8.9). While the true Christian acknowledges the test sent to him by God, these modern 'Neostoics' pretend to deny the existence of such suffering altogether. Whatever its origins, the term 'Neostoicism' has come to refer to the sixteenth and seventeenth century intellectual movement which attempted to revive ancient Stoic philosophy in a form that would be compatible with Christianity. As Calvin's objection attests, this was often seen by others to be a very difficult, if not impossible, task. It is also important to stress that this attempt was not merely to revive scholarly interest in ancient Stoic thought (although it often involved this as well) but rather to revive Stoicism as a living philosophical movement by which people could lead their lives. Lipsius' *De Constantia*, which may be credited as the inspiration for this movement, was first published in 1584, well after Calvin's reference

to contemporary 'Neostoics'. Whomever Calvin had in mind in his polemic, they did not form part of what is now known as the Neostoic movement. The term's use now reflects modern scholarly classification rather than Renaissance self-description. See also Moreau (1999b).

11. See the Preface dedicated to the Consuls, Senate, and People of Antwerp (Latin in Du Bois, 110; English in Kirk, 203).

12. ibid.

13. For Lipsius' life see Aubertus Miraeus, *Vita Justi Lipsi*, in *Opera* 1,7-39; Zanta (1914), 151-66; Saunders (1955), 3-58; Copenhaver and Schmitt (1992), 263-69. For general studies of his life and works see also Anderton (1922b); Gerlo (1988); Morford (1991); Lagrée (1994) and (2004); Laureys (1998); Papy (2004); Cooper (2004).

14. On Plantin (and his relationship with Lipsius) see Clair (1960). Plantin died in 1589, at which point his firm passed into the hands of his son-in-law Joannes Moretus and the firm became 'Plantin-Moretus'.

15. This painting has been dated to *c.* 1611-12 or *c.* 1615, but, either way, after Lipsius' death in 1606. There is also a copy in the Plantin-Moretus Museum, Antwerp. For discussions see Prinz (1973), 418-23; Vlieghe (1987), 128-32; Morford (1991), 3-13.

16. See Montaigne, *Essais* 2.12 (Thibaudet and Rat, 562; Frame, 529). Lipsius and Montaigne also corresponded with each other. Some of Lipsius' letters to Montaigne survive; see Lipsius, *Opera* 2,163; 2,175-6; 2,204. However none of Montaigne's letters to Lipsius survive (on which see Frame, 1273).

17. All of Lipsius' works are gathered together in his *Opera Omnia* of 1637. Another edition appeared in 1675. Full bibliographical details for all of his works can be found in Van Der Haeghen (1886). A useful chronological list may be found in Van De Bilt (1946), 101-03.

18. See *Opera* 1,195-306, although the edition printed there is in only 3 books.

19. See *Opera*, vol. 2. A new critical edition of his letters is currently underway; see Gerlo *et al.* (1978-).

20. *Politicorum sive Civilis Doctrinae Libri Sex* (Leiden: Plantin, 1589). It was translated into English by William Jones as *Sixe Bookes of Politickes or Civil Doctrine* (London, 1594), available in a facsimile reprint (Amsterdam: Theatrum Orbis Terrarum, 1970). There is now a new edition and translation by Waszink. For further discussion see Moss (1998) and Senellart (1999).

21. *Pol.* 1.1.

22. *Pol.* 2.3.

23. From its first publication in 1584 until 1705 there were 32 Latin

editions; see Van Der Haeghen (1886), 73-138. (But in the subsequent three centuries there have been just 2 editions of the Latin text, in 1873 and 1998.) It was also translated into Dutch in 1584 (ibid. 139), French in 1584 (ibid. 147), German in 1599 (ibid. 159), Polish in 1600 (ibid. 171), and Spanish in 1616 (ibid. 169), as well as Stradling's English edition in 1595. For a summary of the vernacular editions see also Van De Bilt (1946), 106-08.

24. Beyond Stradling's 1595 edition, three other English versions were published, in 1653, 1654, and 1670. For full details see below, p. 22. Note also that Kirk dates Stradling's translation to 1594. However, the copy that I have consulted in the British Library is dated 1595.

25. For previous analyses of the text see Zanta (1914), 167-83; Spanneut (1973), 239-41; Oestreich (1982), 13-27.

26. *Const.* 1.2; compare with Epictetus, *Enchiridion* 5.

27. *Const.* 1.2, following Seneca, *Epistulae* 28.2; 104.7. It also appeared four years earlier in the 1580 edition of Montaigne's *Essais* 1.39 (Thibaudet and Rat, 234; Frame, 213).

28. *Const.* 1.3: *Illum mutes oportet, non locum.*

29. *Const.* 1.4: *rectum et immotum animi robur, non elati externis aut fortuitis, non depressi.*

30. *Const.* 1.4: *Rerum quaecunque homini aliunde accidunt aut incidunt volontariam et sine querela perpessionem.*

31. *Const.* 1.6: *immunis a jugo Adfectuum et Fortunae.*

32. It is worth noting that, of these four arguments, three appear in Seneca's 107th letter, a letter that Lipsius described as good and wise (*Senecae Opera*, 631; Morford (1991), 162, reports that Lipsius admired this particular letter). Seneca tells his recipient Lucilius that troubles and neither unusual nor unexpected (Lipsius' fourth argument), that they are inevitable and necessary (Lipsius' second argument), and that it is necessary to follow the will of God under which all events proceed (Lipsius' first argument). Lipsius' third argument can also be found in Seneca, notably his *De Providentia.*

33. Chapters 1-5 of Book Two form an interlude. The first three are devoted to Langius' garden as a place of retreat. The remaining two emphasise that the task at hand is philosophical rather than philological; it is a question of cultivating wisdom rather than mere learning.

34. *Const.* 1.14. For the Stoic dog-cart analogy see Hippolytus, *Refutatio* 1.21 (= *SVF* 2.975). Hippolytus credits this to both Zeno and Chrysippus. See also Cleanthes *apud* Epictetus, *Enchiridion* 53 (= *SVF* 1.527). For discussion see Bobzien (1998), 345-57.

35. *Const.* 1.14, quoting Seneca, *De Vita Beata* 15.7.

36. *Const.* 1.16: *abeunt omnia in hunc nascendi pereundique fatalem gyrum.*
37. *Const.* 1.20. Stoic determinism is itself built upon Stoic materialism, which affirms that only bodies exist. These bodies act as causes and so anything that acts, including the soul, must be corporeal. Aulus Gellius reports that the Stoic Chrysippus defined fate as a natural and everlasting order of causes in which each event follows from another in an unalterable interconnection (*Noctes Atticae* 7.2.3 = *SVF* 2.1000). Thus, as Cicero notes, the Stoic doctrine of fate, conceived as an order and sequence of material causes, is 'not the fate of superstition but rather that of physics' (*De Divinatione* 1.126 = *SVF* 2.921). By rejecting this doctrine, Lipsius attempts to disengage the Stoic ethical ideas to which he is drawn from their foundations in Stoic physics. This is absolutely essential if he is to be able to present Stoic ethics in a form acceptable to a Christian audience. For further discussion see Marin (1988), 122-24 and Lagrée (1999a), 79-82.
38. Later, in *Phys.* 1.12, Lipsius demonstrates a more thorough understanding of the Stoic theory of fate, on the basis of which he suggests that it can in fact be reconciled with Christian doctrine. In order to do this he draws upon Augustine's discussion of Stoic definitions of fate in *De Civitate Dei* 5.8 (part = *SVF* 2.932). Fate does not impinge on the power of God; rather it is the expression of the will of God. For further discussion see Saunders (1955), 54-55.
39. *Const.* 1.22.
40. *Const.* 2.8. It should be noted that these apparently Christian arguments can also be found in Seneca's *De Providentia.*
41. *Const.* 2.18: *quoniam non dubie aequius libentiusque Clades has feremus, persuasi eas non iniquas.*
42. *Const.* 2.21-24.
43. *Const.* 2.26.
44. *Const.* 2.27, with 1.6. For an ancient account of the distinction between *perturbationes (pathê)* and *constantiae (eupatheiai)* see Cicero, *Tusculanae Disputationes* 4.11-14, with Lagrée (1999b), 95-97.
45. *Manuductionis ad Stoicam Philosophiam Libri Tres, L. Annaeo Senecae, aliisque scriptoribus illustrandis* (Antwerp: Plaintin-Moretus, 1604); extracts reprinted and translated into French in Lagrée (1994); extracts also translated into English in Young (1997). *Physiologiae Stoicorum Libri Tres, L. Annaeo Senecae, aliisque scriptoribus illustrandis* (Antwerp: Plantin-Moretus, 1604); extracts reprinted and translated into French in Lagrée (1994). For further discussion see Saunders (1955), which focuses primarily on these two later works and does not examine *De Constantia* in any depth.

46. See Augustine, *De Civitate Dei* 5.8 (part = *SVF* 2.932).
47. *Annaei Senecae Philosophi Opera, Quae Existant Omnia*, A Iusto Lipsio emendata, et Scholiis illustrata (Antwerp: Plantin-Moretus, 1605). Lipsius' *Life of Seneca* and his summaries prefacing each text are translated by Thomas Lodge in his *The Workes of Lucius Annaeus Seneca* (London, 1620), which is based upon Lipsius' edition.
48. See n. 23 above.
49. For surveys of the influence of Lipsius – and the impact of Stoicism more widely – see Zanta (1914); Spanneut (1973), 238-54; Eymard d'Angers (1976); Schmitt *et al.* (1988), 370-74; Moreau (1999a). Interest in Stoicism in the wake of Lipsius appears to have been especially strong in England, and the impact of his revival of Stoicism can be seen in much of English literature of the period; see e.g. Monsarrat (1984); McCrea (1997); Barbour (1998); Shifflett (1998). Lipsius' influence on the development of modern moral philosophy is now being taken increasingly seriously; see Schneewind (1998), 170-75.
50. On this term see n. 10 above.
51. Translated into English as *A Buckler Against Adversitie or A Treatise of Constance* by Andrew Court and published in London in 1622.
52. For the French text see the edition by Michaut. For an English translation see *The Moral Philosophie of the Stoicks*, translated by Thomas James in 1598 (and reissued by Kirk in 1951). An extract is reprinted in Schneewind (2003), 201-15.
53. On Charron's relationship with scepticism see Popkin (1979), 55-62.
54. Translated into English by George Stanhope as *Of Wisdom* in 1697.
55. Charron, *De la sagesse* 3.2.Pref.
56. Charron, *De la sagesse* 1.18.Pref.
57. For an introduction to Quevedo, see Ettinghausen (1972) and note also Méchoulan (1999).
58. The full title is *Nombre, Origen, Intento, Recomendación y Descendencia de la Doctrina Estoica*. There is an English translation in Deitz and Wiehe-Deitz (1997).
59. See Van Der Haeghen (1886), 169.
60. See Deitz and Wiehe-Deitz (1997), 210.
61. ibid. 222.
62. For discussion see Holyoake (1983), 53-58.
63. Montaigne, *Essais* 2.12 (Thibaudet and Rat, 562; Frame, 529).
64. Montaigne, *Essais* 3.10 (Thibaudet and Rat, 997; Frame, 949).
65. See e.g. Blaise Pascal's *Discussion with Monsieur De Sacy*, which deals with Epictetus and with Montaigne's image of Stoicism, in Pascal (1995), 182-92.

66. See e.g. John Bramhall's *Discourse of Liberty and Necessity*, in Chappell (1999), 4-9. This text is especially relevant in the present context because it criticises Lipsius and the 'stoical Christians' who deny any liberty to God. For a general discussion see Brooke (2004).

67. Spinoza's principal works – *Tractatus Theologico-Politicus* and *Opera Posthuma* – were first published in 1670 and 1677 respectively.

68. For modern discussions of Spinoza's relationship with Stoicism see e.g. Kristeller (1984); James (1993); Matheron (1999); Long (2003).

69. See e.g. Giambattista Vico, *The New Science*, § 335 (Vico (1984), 98), who describes the Stoics as 'the Spinozists of their day'. Note also the assessment of Johann Franz Buddeus, in his *De Spinozismo ante Spinozam*, §§ 18-19 (Buddeus (1724), 340-44) and *De Atheismo et Superstitione*, ch. 1 § 18 (Buddeus (1737), 36-39).

70. See for example Pierre Bayle, *Historical and Critical Dictionary*, 'Jupiter', note 'n' (Bayle (1991), 117), where he denounces Stoicism as 'a materialistic atheism'.

71. Diderot (1751-65), vol. 15, 528.

72. For an example of this new methodological approach to Stoicism see Jacob Brucker's *Historia Critica Philosophiae*, abridged and translated in Enfield (1819), vol. 1, 323: 'Great care should be taken, in the first place, not to judge of the doctrine of the Stoics from words and sentiments, detached from the general system, but to consider them as they stand related to the whole train of premises and conclusions. For want of this caution, many moderns, dazzled by the splendid expressions which they have met with in the writings of the Stoics concerning God, the soul, and other subjects, have imagined that they have discovered an invaluable treasure: whereas, if they had taken the pains to restore these brilliants to their proper places in the general mass, it would soon have appeared, that a great part of their value was imaginary'. The text goes on to suggest (ibid. 324) that the works of Seneca, Epictetus, and Marcus Aurelius are not adequate to illustrate the essential doctrines of Stoicism; to do that one must examine the reports in Cicero, Plutarch, Diogenes Laertius, Sextus Empiricus, Simplicius, and Stobaeus. Lipsius himself is discussed in vol. 2, 424-27.

GUIDE TO LIPSIUS' WORKS

All of Lipsius' works are gathered together in his *Opera Omnia*, printed in 4 folio volumes (Antwerp, 1637), and later printed in 4 octavo volumes (Wesel, 1675). The latter has recently been reprinted in a facsimile edition by Georg Olms (4 vols in 8, Hildesheim, 2003). His four works of most interest in the present context (*Const.*, *Pol.*, *Man.*, *Phys.*) are, in both cases, all to be found in volume 4.

The definitive guide to the publishing history of Lipsius' works is Van Der Haeghen (1886). For a useful chronological list see Van De Bilt (1946), 101-03.

De Constantia

The details for the first edition are:

> *Iusti Lipsi De Constantia Libri Duo, Qui alloquium praecipue continent in Publicis malis* (Leiden: Plantin, 1584)

For a comprehensive list of early editions see Van Der Haeghen (1886), vol. 1, 71-177. See also the list in Van De Bilt (1946), 105-06. Editions were issued in 1584, 1585, 1586, 1589, 1590, 1591, 1592, 1594, 1596, 1599, 1601, 1602, 1605, 1613, 1615, 1621, 1624, 1628, 1652, 1680, and 1705. More recent editions of the Latin text include:

> *Traité de la constance*, Traduction nouvelle précédée d'une notice sur Juste Lipse par Lucien Du Bois (Brussels & Leipzig: Merzbach, 1873), with a facing French translation
>
> *De Constantia, Von der Standhaftigkeit: Lateinisch – Deutsch*, Übersetzt, kommentiert und mit einem Nachwort von Florian Neumann, Excerpta Classica 16 (Mainz: Dieterich'sche Verlagsbuchhandlung, 1998), with a facing German translation.

Extracts (*Const.* 1.13-22) are also printed with a facing French translation in Lagrée (1994), 124-59.

The details for Stradling and the other early English translations are:

> *Two Bookes of Constancie*, Written in Latine by Iustus Lipsius [...] Englished by Iohn Stradling (London, 1595)
>
> *Two Books of Constancy*, By Justus Lipsius (London, 1653), attributed by Kirk to Thomas Coningsby; I have not been able to see a copy of this work
>
> *A Discourse of Constancy, in Two Books*, Written in Latin by Justus Lipsius [...] And now faithfully Rendered into English by R. G. (London, 1654)
>
> *A Discourse of Constancy, in Two Books, Chiefly containing Consolations Against Publick Evils*, Written in Latin by Justus Lipsius, and translated into English by Nathaniel Wanley (London, 1670)

Stradling is reprinted with an Introduction and notes by Kirk:

> *Two Bookes of Constancie Written in Latine by Iustus Lipsius*, Englished by Sir John Stradling, Edited with an Introduction by Rudolf Kirk (New Brunswick: Rutgers University Press, 1939)

A short extract (*Const.* 2.1-3) is also translated in Anderton (1922a).

Politica

The original edition is:

> *Politicorum sive Civilis Doctrinae Libri Sex* (Leiden: Plantin, 1589)

It was translated into English shortly afterwards:

> *Sixe Bookes of Politickes or Civil Doctrine*, Done into English by William Jones (London: Richard Field, 1594), with a facsimile edition (Amsterdam: Theatrum Orbis Terrarum, 1970)

There is now a new edition of the text with a facing English translation:

> *Politica: Six Books of Politics or Political Instruction*, Edited, with Translation and Introduction, by Jan Waszink, Bibliotheca Latinitatis Novae 5 (Assen: Royal Van Gorcum, 2004)

Manuductio

The details of the first edition are:

> *Manuductionis ad Stoicam Philosophiam Libri Tres, L. Annaeo Senecae, aliisque scriptoribus illustrandis* (Antwerp: Plaintin-Moretus, 1604)

To the best of my knowledge, the most recent edition is printed in Seneca's *Opera Philosophica*, ed. M.N. Bouillet, 5 vols (Paris, 1827-32), vol. 1, li-ccxliii.

Extracts (*Man.* 2.11-20) are printed with a facing French translation in Lagrée (1994), 160-205; others (*Man.* 2.8, 2.20, 3.6) are translated into English in Young (1997).

A new edition of the text, along with an English translation, by Jill Kraye and Jan Papy is due to be published by the Warburg Institute, London.

Physiologia

The details of the first edition are:

> *Physiologiae Stoicorum Libri Tres, L. Annaeo Senecae, aliisque scriptoribus illustrandis* (Antwerp: Plantin-Moretus, 1604)

To the best of my knowledge, the most recent edition is printed in Seneca's *Opera Philosophica*, ed. M.N. Bouillet, 5 vols (Paris, 1827-32), vol. 4, 481-678.

Extracts (*Phys.* 1.3-12, 3.1) are printed and translated into French in Lagrée (1994), 206-53; another (*Phys.* 1.12) is translated into English in Zanchius (1930), 154-60.

ANALYTIC OUTLINE OF CONTENTS

Book One

1.1-3   **Introductory**: Lipsius travels to escape public evils. Langius says evils are the product of one's opinions and in order to escape evils one must change one's mind, not one's location.

1.4-7   **Constancy introduced**. The antidote to the affections produced by public evils is Constancy. This is the product of Reason, in contrast to Inconstancy, which is the product of Opinion.

1.8-12   **Three enemies of Constancy** are Dissimulation (1.8-10), Piety (1.11), and Pity (1.12).

1.13   **Four arguments outlined** concerning the nature of public evils: they are imposed by God (1.14); the product of Necessity (1.15-22); profitable to us (2.6-17); neither grievous nor unusual (2.18-26).

1.14   **First argument**: Public evils are imposed by God (i.e. the product of Providence).

1.15-22   **Second argument**: Public evils are the product of Necessity (i.e. Fate/Destiny). There are four kinds of Fate (1.17): mathematical; natural; violent (all 1.18); and true (1.19). Four points on which true Fate differs from Stoic violent Fate (1.20). Conclusion of the discussion of Fate (1.21-22).

Book Two

2.1-3   **Interlude** concerning Langius' garden – not a place for Epicurean pleasure but rather for Stoic reflection.

2.4-5   **Warning** against merely discussing Constancy; one must become wise, not merely learned.

2.6-17   **Third argument**: public evils may be profitable (2.6-7). They are profitable in three ways: as exercises for the good

De Constantia

TO THE READER

Reader,[1] I am not ignorant of those new judgements and censures I am likely to undergo in this new way of writing. Partly from such as will be surprised with the unexpected profession of wisdom from him, whom you believed had only been conversant in the more pleasing and delightful studies, and partly from such as will despise and undervalue all that can be said in these matters, after what the ancients have written. To both these it is for my concern, and no less for yours, that I should briefly reply.

The first sort of persons seem to me to miscarry in two most different respects: in their care, and their carelessness. In the former that they assume to themselves a liberty of enquiring into the actions and studies of others; in the latter that their enquiries are yet so overly and superficial. For (that I may give them an account of me) the hills and springs of the Muses did never so entirely possess me that I should not find frequent opportunities to turn back my eyes and mind to that severer deity; I mean Philosophy, the studies of which (even from my childhood) were so pleasing to me that in this youthful kind of ardour I seemed to offend and to stand in need of the bridle of restraint. My tutors at Ubich know how all those kind of books were as it were forced out of my hands together with those writings and commentaries which I had laboriously composed out of all the best ranks of interpreters. Nor certainly did I afterward degenerate, for I know that in all the course of my studies, if not in an exact and straight line, yet as least in the flexure, I have tended towards this mark of wisdom. Not after the rate of most here that deal in Philosophy, who doting upon some thorny subtleties or snares of questions do nothing else but weave and unweave them with a kind of subtle thread of disputations. They rest in words and some little fallacies, and wear away their days in the porch of Philosophy, but never visit its more retired apartments. They use it as a divertissement, not as a remedy, and turn the most

28

serious instrument of life into a sportage with trifles. Who among them seeks after the improvement of his manners, the moderation of his affections, or designs a just end and measure for his fears or hopes? Yes, they suppose that wisdom is so little concerned with these things that they think they do nothing, or nothing to the purpose that look after them. And therefore if you consider their life and sentiments, among the vulgar themselves you will find nothing more foul than this one, nor more foolish than the other. For as wine – though nothing is more wholesome – is yet to some no better than poison, so is Philosophy to those that abuse it. But my mind was otherwise, who always steering my ship from this quick sands of subtleties have directed all my endeavours to attain that one haven of a peaceable and quiet mind. Of which study of mine, I mean these books as the first and undeceivable instance.

But, say some others, these things have been more fully and better treated by the ancients. As to some of them I confess it; as to all I deny it. Should I write any thing of manners or the affections after Seneca and the divine Epictetus, I should have (myself being judge) as little discretion as modesty. But if such things as they have not so much as touched upon, nor any other of the ancients (for I dare confidently affirm it) then why do they despise it, or why do they carp at it? I have sought out consolations against public evils. Who has done it before me? Whether they look upon the matter or the method, they must confess they are indebted to me for both. And for the words themselves (let me say it) we have no such penury as to oblige us to become suppliants to any man.

To conclude, let them understand I have written many other things for others, but this book chiefly for myself; the former for fame, but this for profit. That which one before said bravely and acutely, the same I now truly proclaim. To me a few readers are enough, one is enough, none is enough. All that I desire is that whoever opens this book may bring with him a disposition to profit, and also to pardon. That if possibly I have anywhere slipped (especially when I endeavour to climb those steep places of Providence, Justice, and Fate) they would pardon me. For certainly I have nowhere erred out of malice and obstinacy, but rather through human ignorance and infirmity. To conclude, I desire to be informed by them and I promise that no man shall be so ready to convince as I to correct. The other frailties of my nature I neither dissemble nor extenuate, but obstinacy and the study of contention I do heartily pray I may never be guilty of, and I do detest it. God send you good health, my reader, which I wish may be in part to you through this book.

BOOK ONE

Chapter 1

*A preface and introduction; also a complaint of the troubles of
the Low Countries*

A few years past, as I travelled towards Vienna in Austria, I turned
aside, not without God's direction, to the town of Liege, being not
far out of my way, and where I had some friends, whom both for
custom and good will I was persuaded to salute. Among whom was
Charles Languis, a man, simply and without boasting be it spoken,
for virtue and learning the chief of the Flemings. Who having
received me into his house, tempered my entertainment, not only
with courtesy and good will, but also with such communication as
was profitable to me, and will be while I live. For he was the man
that opened my eyes by driving away the clouds of some vulgar
opinions: he showed me the pathway whereby I might directly
come, as Lucretius says,

> To the lofty temples of Sages right,
> By the clear beams of Learning's light.[2]

For, as we walked in the porch of his house after noon, the hot
sun towards the end of June being in his full force, he asked me
friendly of my journey, and the causes thereof. To whom when I
had spoken much of the troubles of the Low Countries, of the
insolence of the government and soldiers, I added lastly that I
pretended other excuses, but this in truth was the cause of my
departure. For, said I, who is of so hard and flinty a heart that he
can any longer endure these evils? We are tossed, as you see, these
many years with the tempest of civil wars: and like sea-faring men
are we beaten with sundry blasts of troubles and sedition. If I love

quietness and rest, the trumpets and rattling of armour interrupts
me. If I take solace in my country gardens and farms, the soldiers
and murderers force me into the town. Therefore, Langius, I am
resolved, leaving this unfortunate and unhappy Belgica (pardon me
my dear country) to change 'land for land',[3] and to fly into some
other part of the world, where I may neither hear of the name, nor
facts of a Pelops brood.[4]

At this Langius much marvelling and moved said: 'Yes, friend
Lipsius, and will you thus leave us?' 'Yes truly (said I) I will either
leave you, or this life. How can I fly from these evils but only by
flight? For to see and suffer these things daily as heretofore, I
cannot, Langius; neither have I any plate of steel about my heart.'
Langius sighed at these words, and therewithal said to me, 'O fond
youth, what childishness is this? Or what leads you to seek safety
by flying away? Your country, I confess, is tossed and turmoiled
grievously; what part of Europe is at this day free? So as you may
conjecture that saying of Aristophanes to prove true:

Thundering Jupiter will turn all things upside down.[5]

Wherefore, Lipsius, you must not forsake your country, but your
affections.[6] Our minds must be so confirmed and conformed that
we may be at rest in troubles, and have peace even in the midst of
war.' To this I, rashly enough, replied: 'But surely I will forsake my
country, knowing that it is less grief to hear report of evils than to
be an eyewitness to them. Besides that, thereby we ourselves shall
be without danger of the lists. Mark you not what Homer wisely
warns?

Be out of the weapon's reach; lest that happily some
man add one wound to another.'[7]

Chapter 2

That travelling into foreign countries is not available against the inward maladies of the mind; that it is a testimony of them, but not a remedy against them, except only in slight and first motions of the affection.

Langius beckoning somewhat with his head: 'I hear you, Lipsius, but I had rather you would listen to the voice of wisdom and reason. For these mists and clouds that thus surround you, do proceed from the smoke of opinions. Wherefore, I say with Diogenes, you have more need of reason than of a rope;[8] that bright beam of reason, I mean, which may illuminate the obscurity of your brain. Behold, you forsake your country; tell me in good truth, in forsaking it, can you forsake yourself also? See that the contrary not fall out, and that wherever you go you carry not in your breast the fountain and food of your own grief. As they that be held with a fever do toss and turn themselves unquietly, and often change their beds through a vain hope of remedy, in like case are we, who being sick in our minds do without any fruit wander from one country to another. This is indeed to display our grief, but not to allay it. To discover this inward flame, but not to quench it, very fitly said that wise Roman: 'it is proper to a sick person not to suffer anything long, but to use mutations instead of medicines. From here proceed wandering travels, and walks on sundry shores. And our inconstancy, always loathing things present, one whiles will be upon the sea, and incontinent desires the land'.[9] Therefore you fly from troubles always, but never escape them, not unlike the deer that Virgil speaks of:

> Whom ranging through the chase, some hunter shooting far by chance
> All unaware has smit, and in her side has left his lance,
> She fast to wilderness and woods does draw, and there complains,[10]

but all in vain, because as the poet adds,

> That underneath her ribs the deadly dart remains.[11]

So you that are wounded with this dart of affections, do not shake it out, but in travelling carry it with you to another place. He that has broken his thigh or his arm is not inclined, I think, to go on horseback or into his chariot, but to a surgeon. And what madness is this in you, to seek remedy of this inward wound by motion and trudging from place to place?

It is the mind that is wounded, and all this external imbecility, despair, and languishing, spring from this fountain, that the mind is thus prostrated and cast down. The principal and sovereign part has let the sceptre fall and has become so vile and abject that it willingly serves its own servants. Tell me, what good can any place or travel work in this case? Except happily there be some region in the world which can temper fear, bridle hope, and draw out these evil dregs of vice, which we have sucked from our infancy. But none such is there, no not in the fortunate islands. Or if there be, show it to us, and we will all hasten there in troupes.

But you will say that the same mutation and change has that force in it, and that the daily beholding of strange fashions, men, and places does refresh and lighten the mind loaded with oppressions. No, Lipsius, you are deceived. For, to tell you the truth plainly, I do not so much derogate from travelling as though it bare no sway over men and their affections. Yes truly it avails, but yet thus far to the expelling of some small tediousness and weariness of our minds, not to the curing of maladies rooted so deeply, as that these external medicines cannot pluck them out. Music, wine, and sleep have often quenched the first enkindled sparks of anger, sorrow, and love, but they have never weeded out any settled or deep-rooted grief. Likewise I say that travelling might perhaps cure superficial scars, but not substantial sores. For these first motions, having their origin from the body, do stick in the body, or at the most do but cleave to the outer skin of the mind (as a man may say). And therefore no marvel is it, though with a sponge they be lightly washed away, otherwise it is of old festered affections, which hold their seat, and sceptre in the castle of the mind. When you have gone far, and wandered every sea and shore, you will neither drown them in the deep sea, nor bury them in the bowels of the earth. They will follow you at an inch, and, as the poet says, foul care will sit close in the skirts of footman and horseman.[12]

Someone demanded of Socrates how it came to pass that his travelling did him no good. 'Because', said he, 'you forsook not your self'.[13] So say I, that wherever you flee, you carry with you a corrupt mind, a no good companion. And I would pray to God that it were but as your companion, I fear lest it be your captain, in that your affections follow not you, but you them.'

Chapter 3

But deep settled diseases of the mind are not taken away thereby, no nor any way mitigated, but rather revived. That it is the mind which is sick in us, which must seek remedy from wisdom and constancy.

'You will say then, what? Does travelling detract nothing at all from these great evils? Does not the sight of fair fields, rivers, and mountains put a man out of his pains? It may be that they withdraw us from them, but yet for a very short time, and to no good end. Even as a picture be it never so exquisite, delights the eye a little while; so all this variety of persons and places pleases us with the novelty, yet but only for a short season. This is a certain declining from evils, but no avoiding of them. And travelling may well be said to slack the bands of sorrow, but not to lose them. What does it benefit me to behold the sun for a season, and immediately to be shut up in a close prison? So it comes to pass that these external pleasures do beguile the mind, and under pretence of helping do greatly hurt us.

Like as medicines that are weak in operation do not purge ill humours, but provoke them, so these vain delights do kindle and inflame in us the fuel of affections. The mind strays not long from itself, but whether it will or not, is soon driven home to its old harbour of adversities. Those very towns and hills which you will behold for your comfort will reduce you in conceit into your own country. And even in the midst of your joys you will either see or hear something that will rub raw the old gall of your griefs, or else if it be so that you take your ease a while, it will be but short as a slumber, and when you awake your fever will be as it was, or more fervent. For we see that some lusts do increase by intermitting them and by delays gather deeper root. Therefore, Lipsius, let pass these vain, harmful, not remedies, but poisons; and be content to endure the true curing corrasives. Would you willingly change countries? No, rather change your own mind wrongfully subjected to affections, and withdrawn from the natural obedience of its lawful lady, I mean Reason. The corruption and defiling of which causes in you this despair and languishing. The mind must be changed, not the place; and you should transform yourself into another manner of man, not into another place. You have an earnest desire to see the fruitful country of Austria, the good strong town of Vienna, Danube the chief river, with many other rare novelties which may produce admiration in the hearers. How much better is it that your affections were as firmly settled to the obtaining of wisdom? That you should walk through her fertile fields? That you would search out the very fountain of all human perturbations? That you would erect forts and bulwarks wherever you might be able to withstand and repulse the furious assaults of lusts? These be the true remedies of your disease, all the others do but feed and foster the same. Thus your wandering into other countries shall not avail you, it shall nothing benefit you.

> To pass so many towns of Greekish land,
> Or escape by flight through midst of hostile band.[14]

For you will still find an enemy about you, even in that closet of yours. (And there he struck me on the breast.) What good will it do you to be settled in a peaceable place? You carry war with you. What can a quiet habitation benefit you? Troubles are ever about you and in you. For this distracted mind of yours wars, and ever will be at war with itself, in coveting, in flying, in hoping, in despairing. And as they that for fear turn their backs to their enemies are in the greater danger, having their face from their foe, and their backs unarmed, so fares it with these ignorant novices, who never have made any resistance against their affections, but by flight yielded to them. But you, young man, if you be advised by me, will stand to it, and set sure footing against this your adversary, Sorrow. Above all things it befits you to be constant; for by fighting, many a man has gotten the victory, but none by fleeing.'

Chapter 4

The definitions of Constancy, Patience, Right Reason, and Opini.
also how Obstinacy differs from Constancy, and baseness of mi
from Patience.

I being somewhat emboldened with these speeches of Langius, said
to him that truly these admonitions of his were notable and worthy
to be esteemed, and that I began now to lift up myself a little, but
yet in vain, as if it were a man in a slumber. 'For surely, Langius, to
tell you the truth, my thoughts do slide back again to my country,
and the cares of the same, both private and public, are fixed in my
mind. But if you are able, chase away these evil birds that thus feed
upon me, and loose those bands of cares with which I am tied fast
to the Caucasus.'[15]

Hereto Langius with a smiling countenance replied: 'I will drive
them away, and like a newborn Hercules will set at liberty this chained
Prometheus; only give attentive ear to that which I shall say to you.
I have exhorted you to Constancy, and placed in there all hope of
your safety. First, therefore, we must know what it is. "Constancy"
is a right and immovable strength of the mind, neither lifted up nor
pressed down with external or casual accidents.[16] By "strength" I
understand a steadfastness not from Opinion, but from judgement
and sound Reason. For I would in any case exclude obstinacy (or as I
may more correctly term it, pertinacity), which is a certain hardness
of a stubborn mind, proceeding from pride or vainglory. And this
hardness is only in one respect incident to them. For they can hardly
be pressed down but are very easily lifted up, not unlike to a blown
bladder, which you cannot without much ado thrust under water,
but is ready to leap upwards of itself without help. Even such is
the lighthardiness of those men, springing of pride and too much
estimation of themselves, and therefore from Opinion. But the true
mother of Constancy is Patience, and lowliness of mind, which is a
voluntary sufferance without grudging of all things whatsoever can
happen to or in a man.[17] This being regulated by the rule of right
Reason is the very root whereupon is settled the high and mighty
body of that fair oak Constancy. Beware here, lest Opinion beguile
you, presenting to you instead of Patience a certain abjection and

baseness of a dastardly mind. Being a foul vice, proceeding from the vile unworthiness of a man's own person. But virtue keeps the mean, not suffering any excess or defect in her actions, because it weighs all things in the balance of Reason, making it the rule and squire of all her trials. Therefore we define right Reason to be a true sense and judgement of things human and divine (so far as the same pertains to us). But Opinion, being the contrary to it, is defined to be a false and frivolous conjecture of those things.'

Chapter 5

From whence Reason and Opinion do spring. The force and effects of them both. That one leads to Constancy; the other to inconstancy.

'Now for as much as out of this twofold fountain of Opinion and Reason flows not only hardiness and weakness of mind, but all things that deserve either praise or dispraise in this life. It seems to me that it will be labour well bestowed to discourse somewhat at large on the origin and nature of them both. For as wool before it be endued with the perfect colours of dyeing is first prepared with some other kind of liquors, even so am I to deal with your mind, Lipsius, before I adventure to dye it with this perfect purple in grain of Constancy.[18]

First you are not ignorant that man consists of two parts, soul and body. That being the nobler part resembles the nature of a spirit and fire. This more base is compared to the earth. These two are joined together, but yet with a jarring concord, as I may say, neither do they easily agree, especially when controversy arises about sovereignty and subjection. For either of them would bear sway, and chiefly that part which ought not. The earth advances itself above the fire, and the dirty nature above that which is divine. Here hence arise in man dissensions, stirs, and a continual conflict of these parts warring together. The captains are Reason and Opinion. The former fights for the soul, being in the soul; the latter for, and in, the body. Reason has her offspring from heaven, from God, and Seneca gave it a singular commendation, saying "that there was hidden in man part of the divine spirit".[19] This reason is an excellent power or faculty of understanding and judgement, which is the perfection of the soul, even as the soul is of man. The Greeks call it *nous*, the Latins *mens*, and as we may say jointly, the mind of the soul. For you are deceived if you think all the soul to be right Reason, but only that which is uniform, simple, without mixture, separate from all filth or corruption, and in one word, as much as is pure and heavenly. For albeit the soul be infected and a little corrupted with the filth of the body and contagion of the senses. Yet it retains some relics of his first offspring, and is not without certain clear sparks of that pure fiery nature from which it proceeded.

Here hence come those stings of conscience in wicked men, here hence those inward gnawings and scourges, here hence also comes it that the wicked even against their wills approve virtuous living and commend it. For this good part in man may sometimes be pressed down, but never oppressed, and these fiery sparks may be covered, but not wholly extinguished. Those little coals do always shine and show forth themselves, lightening our darkness, purging our uncleanness, directing our doubtfulness, guiding us at the last to Constancy and Virtue. As the marigold and other flowers are by nature always inclined towards the sun, so has Reason a respect for God, and to the fountain from which it sprang. It is resolute and immovable in a good purpose, not variable in judgement, ever shunning or seeking one and the self same thing: the fountain and lively spring of wholesome counsel and sound judgement. To obey is to bear rule, and to be subject to it is to have the sovereignty in all human affairs. Who so obeys her is lord of all lusts and rebellious affections, who so has this thread of Theseus may pass without straying through all the labyrinths of this life.[20] God by this image of his comes to us, even into us. And well said that one, whosoever he were, 'that there is no good mind without God'.[21]

But the other part (I mean Opinion) has its offspring of the body, that is, of the earth, and therefore savours nothing but of it. For though the body be senseless and immovable of itself, yet it takes life and motion from the soul. And on the other side, it represents to the soul the shapes and forms of things through the windows of the senses. Thus there grows a communion and society between the soul and the body, but a society (if you respect the end) not good for the soul. For she is thereby little by little deprived of her dignity, addicted and coupled to the senses, and of this impure co-mixture Opinion is engendered in us, which is nothing else but a vain image and shadow of reason, whose seat is the senses, whose birth is the earth. Therefore being vile and base it tends downwards and savours nothing of high and heavenly matters. It is vain, uncertain, deceitful, evil in counsel, evil in judgement. It deprives the mind of Constancy and Verity. Today it desires a thing, tomorrow it defies the same. It commends this, it condemns that. It has no respect to sound judgement, but to please the body and content the senses. And as the eye that beholds a thing through water or through a mist mistakes it, so does the mind which discerns by the clouds of opinions. This is to men the mother of mischiefs, the author of a confused and troublesome life. By the means of it we are troubled with cares, distracted with perturbations, overruled by vices. Therefore, as they which would banish tyranny out of a city do above all things overthrow castles and forts therein, so if we bear an earnest desire to have a good mind, we must cast down even by the foundation this castle of opinions. For they will cause us to be continually floating on the waves of doubtfulness, without any certain resolution, murmuring, troublesome, injurious to God and men. As an empty ship without ballast is tossed and tumbled on the sea with the least blast of wind, even so is it with a light, wandering mind not kept steady and poised with the ballast of reason.'

Chapter 6

The praise of Constancy, and an earnest exhortation thereto.

'You see then, Lipsius, that inconstancy is the companion of Opinion, and that the property of it is to be soon changed, and to wish that undone which a little before it caused to be done. But Constancy is a mate always matched with Reason. To this therefore I do earnestly exhort you. Why do you fly to these vain outward things? This is only that fair beautiful Helena which will present to you a wholesome cup of counter-poison, with which you will expel the memory of all cares and sorrows, and when you have once taken a taste, being firmly settled against all casualties, bearing yourself upright in all misfortunes, neither puffed up nor pressed down with either fortune, you may challenge to yourself that great title, the nearest that man can have to God, to be immovable.

Have you not seen in the arms and targets of some men of our time that lofty poetry "neither with hope, nor with fear"? It will agree to you. You will be a king indeed, free indeed, only subject to God, enfranchised from the servile yoke of fortune and affections. As some rivers are said to run through the sea and yet keep their stream fresh, so will you pass through the confused tumults of this world and not be infected with any briny saltiness of this sea of sorrows. Are you likely to be cast down? Constancy will lift you up. Do you stagger in doubtfulness? She holds you fast. Are you in danger of fire or water? She will comfort you and bring you back from the pit's brink. Only take to yourself a good courage, steer your ship into this port, where there is security and quietness, a refuge and sanctuary against all turmoils and troubles, where if you have once moored your ship, let your country not only be troubled but even shaken at the foundation, you will remain unmoved. Let showers, thunder, lightning, and tempests fall round about you, you will cry boldly with a loud voice, "I lie at rest amid the waves".'

Chapter 7

What and how many things do disturb Constancy. That outward good and evil things do it. Evils are of two sorts, public and private. Of these two, public evils seem more grievous and dangerous.

Langius having uttered these words with a more earnest voice and countenance than accustomed, I was somewhat enflamed with a spark of this good fire. And then, 'my father', I said, '(let me rightly without dissimulation call you so), lead me and learn me as you list; direct and correct me; I am your patient prepared to admit any kind of curing, be it by razor or fire, to cut or sear'. 'I must use both those means', said Langius, 'for that one while the stubble of false opinions is to be burned away, and another while the tender slips of affections to be cut off by the root. But tell me whether had you rather walk or sit?' 'Sitting would please me best', said I, 'for I begin to be hot'. So then Langius commanded stools to be brought into the porch, and I sitting close by him, he turned himself towards me and began his talk in this manner.

'So far, Lipsius, I have laid the foundation whereupon I might erect the building of my future communication. Now, if it please you, I will come nearer the matter and enquire into the causes of your sorrow, for I must touch the sore with my hand. There be two things that do assault this castle of Constancy in us, false goods and false evils. I define them both to be such things as are not in us but about us, and which properly do not help nor hurt the inner man, that is, the mind. Therefore I may not call those things good or evil simply in subject and in definition, but I confess they are such in opinion and by the judgement of the common people. In the first rank[22] I place riches, honour, authority, health, long life. In the second[23] poverty, infamy, lack of promotion, sickness, death. And to comprehend all in one word, whatsoever else is accidental and happens outwardly.

From these two roots do spring four principal affections which do greatly disquiet the life of man: Desire and Joy, Fear and Sorrow.[24] The first two have respect to some supposed or imagined good, the latter two to evil. All of them do hurt and distemper the mind, and without timely prevention do bring it out of all order, yet not each of them in the same way. For whereas the quietness and constancy of the mind rests, as it were, in an even balance, these affections do hinder this upright poise and evenness; some of them by puffing up the mind, others by pressing it down too much. But here I shall let pass to speak of false goods which lift up the mind above measure, because your disease proceeds from another humour, and will come to false evils, which are of two sorts, public and private. Public are those of which the sense and feeling touches many persons at one time. Private do touch some private men. Of the first kind are war, pestilence, famine, tyranny, slaughters, and such like. Of the second be sorrow, poverty, infamy, death, and whatsoever else of like nature that may befall any one man.

I take it there is good cause for me thus to distinguish them, because we sorrow after another sort at the misery of our country, the banishment and destruction of a multitude, than of one person alone. Besides that, the griefs that grow of public and private adversities are different, but yet the first sort are more heavy and take deeper root in us. For we are all subject to those common calamities, either for that they come together in heaps, and so with the multitude oppress such as oppose themselves against them, or rather because they beguile us by subtlety, in that we perceive not how our mind is diseased by the apprehension of them. Behold if a man be overcome with any private grief, he must confess therein his frailty and infirmity, especially if he reclaim not himself, then is he without excuse. Contrarily, we are so far from confessing a fault in being disquieted at public calamities that some will boast thereof and account it for a praise: for they term it piety and compassion. So that this common contagion is now reckoned among the catalogue of virtues, and almost honoured as a God. Poets and orators do everywhere extol to the skies a fervent affection to our country; neither do I disallow it but hold and maintain that it ought to be tempered with moderation, otherwise it is a vice, a note of intemperance, a deposing of the mind from its right seat. On the other side I confess it to be a grievous malady and of great force to move a man, because the sorrow that proceeds from it is manifold, in respect of oneself and of others. And to make the matter more plain by example, see how your country of Belgica is afflicted with sundry calamities and swung on every side with the scorching flame of civil wars: the fields are wasted and spoiled, towns are overthrown and burned, men taken captive and murdered, women defiled, virgins deflowered, with such other like miseries as follow after wars. Are you not grieved with this? Yes I am sure, and grieved diversely, for your self, for your countrymen, and for your country. Your own losses trouble you; the misery and slaughter of your neighbours; the calamity and overthrow of your country. One time you may cry out with the poet, "O unhappy wretch, that I am".[25] Another while, "alas that so many of my countrymen should suffer such affliction by the enemies' hand".[26] Another while, "O my father, O my country".[27] And whosoever is not moved with these matters, nor oppressed with the multitude of so many and manifold miseries, must either be very stayed and wise, or else very hardhearted.'

Chapter 8

A prevention against public evils. But first of all, three affections
are restrained. And of those three, particularly in this chapter is
repressed a kind of vainglorious dissimulation, whereby men that
lament their own private misfortunes would seem that they bewail
the common calamities.

'What do you think, Lipsius, have I not betrayed Constancy into your
hands in pleading the cause of your sorrow? Not so. But so far I
have played the part of a good captain, in training out all your troops
into the field to the end that I might fight it out manfully with them.
But first I will begin with light skirmishes and afterwards join with
you in plain battle. In skirmishing I am to assault foot by foot, as the
ancients speak, three affections utter enemies to this, our Constancy:
dissimulation, piety, commiseration or pity.[28] I will begin with the first
of them. You say that you cannot endure to see these public miseries,
that it is a grief, even a death to you. Do you speak that from your
heart, or only from the teeth outward?' At this I, being somewhat
angry, asked whether he jested or gibed with me. 'No', said Langius.
'I speak in good earnest for that many of your crew do beguile the
physicians, making them believe that the public evils do grieve them
when their private losses are the true cause. I demand therefore again
whether the care "which now does boil and bubble in your breast",[29]
be for your country's sake or for your own?' 'Why', said I, 'do you
make question of that? Surely, Langius, for my country's sake alone
am I thus disquieted'. 'See it be so', said he, 'for I marvel that there
should be in you such an excellent sincere duty to which few attain.
I deny not but that most men do complain of common calamities,
neither is there any kind of sorrow so usual as this in the tongues
of people. But examine the matter to the quick, and you shall find
many times great difference between the tongue and the heart. Those
words, "my country's calamity afflicts me", carry with them more
vainglory than verity. And as it is recorded in histories of Polus a
notable stage-player, that playing his part on the stage in which he
was required to express some great sorrow, he brought with him the
bones of his dead son, and so the remembrance thereof caused him
to fill the theatre with true tears indeed.[30] Even so may I say by the

most part of you. You play a comedy, and under the person of your country, you bewail with tears your private miseries. One says "the whole world is a stage-play". Truly in this case it is so. Some cry out, "these civil wars torment us, the blood of innocents spilt, the loss of laws and liberty". Is it so? I see your sorrow indeed, but the cause I must search out more narrowly. Is it for the commonwealth's sake? O player, put off your mask: you are the cause yourself. We see often the country peasants trembling and running together with earnest prayers when any sudden misfortune or insurrection approaches, but as soon as the danger is past, examine them well and you will perceive that every one was afraid for his own field and corn. If fire should happen to be kindled in this city, we should have a general outcry; the lame and almost the blind would hasten to help quench it. What think you? For their country's sake? Ask them and you will see, it was because the loss would have extended to all, or at the least, the fear of it. So it falls out in this case. Public evils do move and disquiet many men, not because the harm touches a great number, but because they themselves are of that number.'

Chapter 9

The mask of dissimulation is more plainly discovered, by examples. By the way mention is made of our true country; also the malice of men rejoicing at other men's harms when they themselves are without danger.

'Wherefore you will sit as judge in this cause, but yet with the veil removed from your face. You fear the war. I know it. Why? Because war draws with it punishment and destruction. To whom? To others at the present, but it may be shortly to you. Behold the head, behold the fountain of your grief. For as a thunderbolt having struck one man makes all that stood near him tremble, so in these universal and public calamities the loss touches few, the fear extends to all, which fear if it were away, there would be no place for sorrow. Behold, if war be among the Ethiopians or Indians, it moves you not (you are out of danger); if it be in Belgica you weep, cry out, rub your forehead, and strike your thigh. But now if it were so that you did bewail the public evils as public, and for themselves, there should be no difference had of you between those countries and this.

You will say, it is not of my country. O fool: are not they men, sprung first out of the same stock with you? Living under the same globe of heaven? Upon the same mold of earth? Do you think that this little plot of ground environed by such and such mountains, compassed with this or that river, is your country? You are deceived. The whole world is our country, wherever the race of mankind is sprung of that celestial seed. Socrates, being asked of what country he was, answered, "of the world".[31] For a high and lofty mind will not suffer itself to be penned by Opinion within such narrow bounds, but conceives and knows the whole world to be its own. We scorn and laugh at fools who suffer their masters to tie them with a straw or small thread to a post where they stand, as if they were fettered fast with iron. Our folly is not inferior to theirs, who with the weak link of Opinion are wedded to one corner of the world.

But to let pass these deep arguments (which I doubt is how you will conceive of them) I demand, if God would assure you in the midst of these broils, that your fields should be unspoiled, your house and substance in safety, and your self on some high mountain placed out of all danger. Would you lament for all this? I am loathed to affirm it of you, but I am certain that there be many that would be glad of it, and feed their eyes greedily with the spectacle of such bloody butcheries. Why do you turn aside? Why do you marvel at this? Such is the natural corruption of man, that, as the poet says, "it rejoices at other men's harms".[32] And as some apples are bitter in the belly yet relishing sweet in taste, so are other men's miseries, we ourselves being free from them. Suppose a man be on the shore beholding a shipwreck, it will move him somewhat, yet truly not without an inward tickling of his mind, because he sees other men's danger, himself being in security. But if he in person were in that distressed ship, he would be touched with another manner of grief. Even so verily is it in this case, let us say, or make what show we list to the contrary. "For we bewail our own misfortunes earnestly and from the heart, but public calamities in words only and for fashion's sake".[33] Wherefore, Lipsius, take away these stage-hangings, draw back the curtain that is in front of you, and without all counterfeiting or dissimulation, acquaint us with the true cause of your sorrow.'

Chapter 10

A complaint against the former sharp reprehension of Langius.
But he adds that it is the part of a philosopher so to speak freely.
He endeavours to confute the former disputation speaking of duty
and love to our country.

This first skirmish seemed to me very hot, wherefore interrupting
him I replied, 'What liberty of speech is this that you use? What
bitter taunting? Do you in this way pinch and prick me? I may well
answer you with Euripides' words,

> Add not more grief to my strong disease,
> I suffer more (God knows) than is my ease.'[34]

Langius smiling at this, 'I perceive then', said he, 'you expect
wafer cakes or sweet wine at my hands; but ever while you desired
either fire or razor, and therein you did well. For I am a philosopher,
Lipsius, not a fiddler: my purpose is to teach, not to entice you; to
profit, not to please you; to make you blush, rather than smile; and
to make you penitent, not insolent. "The school of a philosopher is
as a physician's shop", so said Rufus once,[35] where we must repair
for health, not for pleasure. That physician dallies not, neither
flatters, but pierces, pricks, razes, and with the savoury salt of good
talk sucks out the filthy corruption of the mind. Wherefore do not
look to me for roses, oils, or pepper, but for thorns, lancing tools,
wormwood, and sharp vinegar.'

Here I took him up, saying, 'Truly, Langius, if I may be so bold
as to be plain with you, you deal scarce well or charitably with
me. Neither do you like a stout champion overcome me in lawful
striving, but undermine me by slights and subtleties, saying that
I bewail my country's calamities fainedly, and not for good will
to it, wherein you do me wrong. For let me confess freely that I
have some manner of regard to myself, yet not wholly. I lament
the cause of my country principally, and so will do, although the
danger she is in extends not in any sort to me. There is good reason
why I should do so. For it was she that first received me into this
world, and after that nourished and bred me, being, by common

consent of all nations, our most ancient and holiest mother. But you assign me the whole world for my country. Who denies that? Yet withal you may not gainsay, that besides this large and universal country, there is another more near and dear to me, to which I am tied by a secret bond of nature, except you think there is no virtue persuasive nor attractive in that native soil which we first touched with our bodies and pressed with our feet, where we first drew our breath, where we cried in our infancy, played in our childhood, and exercised ourselves in manhood; where our eyes are acquainted with the firmament, floods, and fields; where have been by a long continuance of descents our kinsfolk, friends, and companions, and to many occasions of joy besides, which I may expect in vain in another part of the world. Neither is all this the slender thread of Opinion, as you would have it seem, but the strong fetters of nature herself. Look upon all other living creatures. The wild beasts do both know and love their dens; and birds their nests. Fishes in the great and endless ocean sea, desire to enjoy some certain part thereof. What need I say about men who, whether they are civil or barbarous, are so addicted to this their native soil that whosoever bears the face of a man will never refuse to die for it and in it. Therefore, Langius, this new found curious philosophy of yours, I neither perceive as yet the depth of it, nor care to make profession thereof. I will listen rather to the true saying of Euripides,

> Necessity forces every wight,
> To love his country with all his might.'[36]

Chapter 11

Here is confuted the second affection of too much love to our country, which is falsely termed piety. Whence this affection springs, and what is our country properly and truly.

Then Langius smiling replied: 'Certain you are a marvellous pious young man, and I fear that the brother of Marcus Antonius is now in danger of being deprived of his surname.[37] But it falls out fitly that this affection offers itself in sallying before his ensign. I will assault him therefore, and overthrow him lightly. And first I shall take from him the spoil of that precious garment with which he is unworthily attired. This affection to our country is commonly called *pietas*, that is Piety. Why it should be so named I neither see nor can suffer it. For why should we call it by the name of Piety, which is an excellent virtue, and properly nothing else but a lawful and due honour and love towards God and our parents? Why should our country be placed in the middle between these? Because, they say, it is our most ancient and holiest mother. O fools, injurious to reason and nature herself, is she our mother? How? Or wherefore? Truly I see no such reason. And if you, Lipsius, if you be sharper sighted than I, lighten my dark senses. Is it because she first received us into this world (for so you seemed to affirm before)? So might any taverner or innkeeper. Is it because she cherishes us? Much better does some silly maid or nurse. Is it because she nourishes us? So do cattle, trees, and corn daily, and (among the greater substances which do borrow nothing of the earth) the firmament, air, and water. Finally, change your habitation, and every other part of the world will do thus much for you. These are floating and fleeting words, savouring of nothing but an unpleasant juice of popular opinion. They alone are our parents that begat, shaped, and bore us. We are the seed of their seed, blood of their blood, and flesh of their flesh. If any of these things belong in any way to our country, then I confess that I go about wrongfully to bereave it of this duty of piety.

You will say that great learned clerics have so spoken of it. They have indeed so spoken, following the common opinion, but not so that they were so persuaded themselves. But if you will follow the truth, you will attribute that sacred and high title to God, and also, if you think good, to our parents. But as for this affection to our country, being first bridled and restrained to a mean, let it be contented in God's name with the title of Love or Charity.

Yet is this only a contention about the name? Let us come nearer to the thing itself, which I do not wholly take away, but temper, and, as it were, cut back with the scalpel of right Reason. For as a vine if it is not pruned, spreads itself too far abroad, so do affections fly about with full sail being blown with the plausible puffs of popularity.

And notwithstanding here by the way I confess – for I am not degenerated from a man, nor from a citizen – I confess, I say, that every one of us has an inclination and good will to his lesser country, the causes of which I perceive are to you unknown. You would have it to be from nature, but the truth is it grows of custom, or of some decree and ordinance. For after men forsook their wild and savage manner of living, and began to build houses and walled towns, to join in society, and to use means offensive and defensive, behold then a certain communion necessarily began among them, and a social participation of diverse things. They parted the earth between them with certain limits and bounds; they had temples in common; also marketplaces, treasuries, seats of judgement; and principally ceremonies, rites, laws. All these things our greediness began in time to esteem and make account of, as if they were our own in particular. And so they be in some sort, for every private citizen had some interest in them; neither did they differ from private possessions, except that they were not wholly in one man's power. This communion and fellowship gave the form and fashion to a new erected state, which now we call properly the commonwealth, or our country. When men saw the chief stay of each person's safety to consist in this, laws were enacted for the succour and defence of it; or at the least such customs were received by tradition from the predecessors to their posterity that grew to be of like force as laws. From this it comes to pass that we rejoice at the good of the commonwealth, and be sorry for her harm – because our own private goods are secure by her safety, and are lost by her overthrow. From this fountain do spring the streams of our goodwill and love towards her, which affection in respect of the common good (the secret providence of God leading thereto) our ancestors increased, by all possible means establishing and maintaining the majesty of their country.

It appears therefore, in my judgement, that this affection had its beginning from custom, and not from nature, as you pretend. Else why should not the same measure of that affection be indifferently in all men? Why should the nobility and rich men have more care of their country than the poor people, who commonly take care for their private matters but none at all for the public affairs? Which thing falls out otherwise in all passions that be governed by the instinct of nature. Finally what reason can you allege that so small and light an occasion should often assuage, even wholly extinguish it? See how every day some for anger, some for love, some for ambition forsake their country? And what a multitude are drawn away by that idol lucre? How many Italians forsaking Italy the queen of countries only for greediness of gain have removed their dwellings into France, Germany, even into Sarmatia? How many thousand Spaniards does ambition draw daily into another world from us? These arguments prove invincibly that the band whereby we are linked thus to our country is but external and accidental, in that it is so easily broken by one inordinate lust.

Moreover, Lipsius, you are greatly deceived in describing this country of ours, for you tie it very narrowly to that native soil where we were born and had our education, with other like frivolous allegations, from whence you labour in vain to pick out natural causes of our affection towards her. And if it be the native soil where we were born that deserves this title of our country then is Brussels only my country, and Iscanum yours; and to some other man, a poor cottage or cell; and to many, not so much as a cottage, but a wood, or else the open field; what then? Shall my good will and affections be shut up within those narrow walls? Shall I settle my disposition and love upon one town or house as my country? What folly were that? You see also that by your description none are happier than those that are born in the woods and open fields, which are always flourishing, and seldom or never be subject to desolation or wasting. No, no, our country is not as you take it, but it is, some one state, or as it were one common ship, under the regiment of one prince, or one law, which I confess we ought to love, to defend, and to die for. Yet must it not drive us to lament, wail and despair. Well said the poet,

> A happy quarrel is it and a good,
> For country's cause to spend our dearest blood.[38]

He said not that we should weep and lament, but die for our country. For we must so far forth be good commonwealth men, that we also retain the person of good and honest men, which we lose if we take to childish and womanlike lamentations.

Last of all, Lipsius, I would have you learn this one hidden and deep mystery, that if we respect the whole nature of man, all these earthly countries are vain and falsely so termed, except only in respect of the body, and not of the mind or soul, which descending down from that highest habitation, deems all the whole earth as a jail or prison, but heaven is our true and rightful country. Let us advance all our thoughts that we may freely say with Anaxagoras to such as foolishly ask us whether we have no regard to our country, "yes verily, but yonder is our country", lifting our finger and mind up towards heaven'.[39]

Chapter 12

The third affection bridled, which is commiseration or pitying, being a vice. It is distinguished from mercy. How and how far forth we ought to use it.

Langius with this conference having scattered abroad some dark mists from my mind, I spoke to him thus. 'My father, what by admonitions and what by instructions you have done me great good, so that it seems that I am now able to moderate my affection towards the native soil or commonwealth where I was born, but not towards the persons of my fellow citizens and countrymen. For how should I not be touched and tormented with the calamities of my country for my countrymen's sake, who are tossed in this sea of adversities, and do perish by sundry misfortunes?' Langius, taking my tale by the end: 'This is not', said he, 'properly sorrow, but rather commiseration or pitying, which must be despised by he who is wise and constant, whom nothing so much suits as steadiness and steadfastness of courage, which he cannot retain if he is cast down not only with his own mishaps, but also at other men's'. 'What Stoical subtleties are these?' said I. 'Will you not have me to pity another man's case? Surely it is a virtue among good men, and such as have any religion in them?'

'I deny that', said Langius, 'and I trust no good man will be offended with me, if I purge the mind of this malady, for it is a very dangerous contagion, and I judge him not far from a pitiful state that is subject to pitying of others. As it is a token of naughty eyes to wax watery when they behold other blear eyes, so is it of the mind that mourns at every other man's mourning. It is defined to be the fault of an abject and base mind, cast down at the show of another's mishap.' 'What then? Are we so unkind and void of humanity that we would have no man to be moved at another's misery?' 'Yes, I allow that we be moved to help them, not to bewail or wail with them. I permit mercy, but not pitying. I call mercy an inclination of the mind to succour the necessity or misery of another. This is that virtue, Lipsius, which you see through a cloud, and instead of which pity intrudes herself into you.

But you will say it is incident to man's nature to be moved with affection and pity. So be it, yet certainly it is not decent and right. Do you think that any virtue consists in softness and abjection of the mind? In sorrowing? In sighing? In sobbing together with such as weep? It cannot be so. For I will show you some greedy old wives and covetous misers from whose eyes you may sooner wring a thousand tears than one small penny out of their purses. But he that is truly merciful in deed will not bemoan or pity the condition of distressed persons but yet will do more to help and succour them than the other. He will behold men's miseries with the eye of compassion yet ruled and guided by reason. He will speak to them with a sad countenance but not mourning or prostrate. He will comfort heartily, and help liberally. He will perform more in works than in words and he will stretch out to the poor and needy his hand rather than his tongue. All this will he do with discretion and care, that he not infect himself with other men's contagion, and that, as fencers used to say, he bear not others' blows upon his own ribs. What is here savouring of inhumanity or churlishness? Even so all wisdom seems austere and rigorous at the first view. But if you consider it thoroughly, you will find the same to be meek, gentle, and even more mild and amiable than Venus herself. Let this suffice touching the three aforementioned affections, whom if I have in part expelled from you, it will greatly avail me to get the victory in the battle that will ensue.'

Chapter 13

The former impediments being removed, we come in good earnest to the extenuating or taking away of public evils, which is assayed by four principal arguments. First here is spoken of Providence, which is proved to be in and over all human affairs.

'I come now from skirmishes to handgrips, and from light bickerings to the main battle. I will lead forth all my soldiers in order, under their ensigns, dividing them into four troops. First I will prove that these public evils are imposed upon us by God himself. Secondly, that they are necessary and by destiny. Thirdly, that they are profitable for us. Finally, that they be neither grievous nor strange.[40] These troops if they discharge their parts each one in his place, can the whole army of your sorrow make any resistance, or once open the mouth against me? No truly, I must have the victory. In token of this sound the trumpets and strike up the drums.

Whereas, Lipsius, all affections that do disturb man's life proceed from a mind distempered and void of reason, yet none of them do more, in my conceit, than that sorrow which is conceived for the commonwealth's sake. For all others have some final cause and scope to which they tend, as the lover to enjoy his desire, the angry man to be avenged, the covetous churl to get, and so forth. Only this has no end proposed to it. And to restrain my talk to some certainty, you, Lipsius, bewail the state of your country decaying. Tell me to what effect? Or what do you hope to obtain thereby? To amend that which is amiss? To preserve that which is about to perish? Or by weeping to take away the plague or punishment that hangs over your country? None of all these, but only that you may say with the common sort, "I am sorry". In all other respects your mourning is in vain and to no purpose. For that thing which is past, God himself would not have to be undone again.

Neither is this weeping of yours, vain only, but also wicked and ungodly, if it is rightly considered. For you know well that there is an eternal spirit, whom we call God, which rules, guides, and governs the rolling spheres of heaven, the manifold courses of the stars and planets, the successive alterations of the elements, and finally, all things whatsoever in heaven and earth. Do you think that chance or fortune bears any sway in this excellent frame of the world? Or that the affairs of mortal men are carried headlong by chance medley? I know well you do not think so, nor any man else that has either wisdom or wit in his head. It is the voice of nature itself, and which way so ever we turn our eyes or minds, all things both mortal and immortal, heavenly and earthly, sensible and insensible, do with open mouth cry out and affirm that there is somewhat far above us that created and formed these so many wonderful works, which also continually governs and preserves the same. This is God, to whose absolute perfection nothing is more agreeable than to be both able and willing to take the care and charge of his own workmanship. And why should he not be willing, seeing that he is the best of all? Why should he not be able, seeing he is the mightiest of all? In so much yet there is no strength above him, nor any but that which proceeds from him, neither is he letted or troubled with the greatness or variety of all these things. For this eternal light casts forth his bright beams everywhere, and in a moment pierces even into the bosom and bottom of the heavens, earth, and sea. It is not only president over all things, but present in them. And no marvel. What a great part of the world does the Sun lighten at once? What a mass of matter can our mind comprehend at once? O fools, cannot he that made this sun and this mind perceive and conceive far more things than they? Well and divinely spoke one that had small skill in divinity: "as is the pilot in a ship, the driver to his wagon, the chanter in a choir, the law in a commonwealth, and the general in an army, so is God in the world. Here is the only difference, that their charge is to them laboursome, grievous, and painful. But God rules without all pain and labour or bodily striving."[41] Wherefore, Lipsius, there is in God a watchful and continual care, yet without burden, whereby he beholds, searches, and knows all things; and knowing them, disposes and orders the same by an immutable course to us unknown. And this is it, which here I call Providence, of which some man through infirmity may grudge or complain, but not doubt, except if he is benumbed of his senses, and besotted against nature.'

Chapter 14

That nothing is here done but by the beck of this Providence.
That by it desolations come upon men and cities; therefore we do
not the parts of good and godly men to murmur or mourn for
them. Finally, an exhortation to obey God against whom we strive
unadvisedly and in vain.

'If you conceive this rightly, and do believe heartily that this
governing faculty insinuates itself, and, as the poet speaks, "passes
through every path of sea and eke of shore",[42] I see not what further
place can be left for your grief and grudging. For even the selfsame
foreseeing intelligence which turns about the heaven daily, which
causes the sun to rise and set, which brings forth and shuts up the
fruits of the earth, produces all these calamities and changes which
you so much marvel and mutter at. Do you think that God gives us
only pleasing and profitable things? No, he sends likewise noisome
and hurtful. Neither is anything contrived, tossed, or turned (sin
only excepted) in this huge theatre of the world, the cause and
fountain of which proceeds not from that first cause of causes, for
as Pindar says well, "the dispensers and doers of all things are in
heaven".[43] And there is let down from this a golden chain (as Homer
expresses by a figment)[44] to which all these inferior things are fast
linked. That the earth has opened her mouth and swallowed up some
towns, came of God's Providence. That elsewhere the plague has
consumed many thousands of people, proceeds of the same cause.
That slaughters, war, and tyranny rage in the Low Countries, from
there it also comes to pass. From heaven, Lipsius, from heaven are
all these miseries sent. Therefore Euripides said it well and wisely,
"that all calamities come from God".[45] The ebbing and flowing of
all human affairs depends upon that moon. The rising and fall of
kingdoms comes from this sun. You therefore in loosening the reins
thus to your sorrow, and grudging that your country is so turned and
overturned, do not consider what you are, and against whom you
complain. What are you? A man, a shadow, dust? Against whom do
you fret? I fear to speak it, even against God.

The ancients have told that giants advanced themselves against
God, to pull him out of his throne.[46] Let us omit these fables. In

very truth you querulous and murmuring men be these giants. For if it be so that God does not only suffer but send all these things, then you who thus strive and struggle, what else do you do but, as much as in you lies, take the sceptre and sway of government from him? O blind mortality. The sun, the moon, stars, elements, and all creatures else in the world do willingly obey that supreme law; only man, the most excellent of all God's works, lifts up his heel and spurns against his maker. If you hoist your sails to the winds, you must follow wherever they will force you, not where your will leads you. And in this great ocean sea of our life will you refuse to follow that breathing spirit which governs the whole world? Yet you strive in vain. For if you follow not freely you will be drawn after forcibly.[47] We may laugh at him who, having tied his boat to a rock, afterwards hauls the rope as though the rock should come to him, when he himself goes nearer to it. But our foolishness is far greater, who being fast bound to the rock of God's eternal providence, by our hailing and pulling would have the same to obey us, and not we it. Let us forsake this fondness, and if we be wise let us follow that power which from above draws us, and let us think it good reason that man should be pleased with that which pleases God. The soldier in camp, having a sign of marching forward given him, takes up all his trinkets; but hearing the note of battle lays them down, preparing and making himself ready with heart, eyes, and ears, to execute whatsoever shall be commanded. So let us in this our warfare follow cheerfully and with courage wherever our general calls us. "We are hereto adjured by oath", says Seneca, "even to endure mortality, nor to be troubled with those things which it is not in our power to avoid. We are born in a kingdom, and to obey God is liberty".[48]

Chapter 15

A passage to the second argument for Constancy, which is taken from necessity. The force and violence thereof, this necessity is considered two ways, and first in the things themselves.

'This is a sure brazen target against all outward accidents. This is that gold armour with which being fenced, Plato willed us to fight against chance and fortune, to be subject to God, to think on God, and in all events to cast our mind upon that great Mind of the world, I mean Providence, whose holy and happy troops having orderly trained forth. I will now bring out another band under the banner of Necessity. A band valiant, strong, and hard as iron, which I may fitly term the thundering legion. The power of this is stern and invincible, which tames and subdues all things. Wherefore, Lipsius, I marvel if you withstand it. Thales, being asked "what was strongest of all things?" answered, "Necessity, for it overcomes all things".[49] And to that purpose there is an old saying, though not so warily spoken, "that the gods cannot constrain Necessity".[50] This Necessity I join next to Providence, because it is near kin to it, or rather born of it. For from God and his decrees necessity springs, and it is nothing else, as the Greek philosopher defines it, but "a firm ordinance and immutable power of Providence".[51] That it has a stroke in all public evils that befall, I will prove two ways: from the nature of things themselves, and from destiny. And first from the things, in that it is a natural property of all things created to fall into mutability and alteration; as to iron cleaves naturally a consuming rust; to wood a gnawing worm, and so a wasting rottenness. Even so to living creatures, cities, and kingdoms, there be certain inward causes of their own decay. Look upon all things high and low, great and small, made with hand, or composed by the mind, they always have decayed, and ever will. And as the rivers with a continual swift course run into the sea, so all human things through this conduit of wastings and calamities slide to the mark of their desolation. Death and destruction is this mark, and the means to come here are plague, war, and slaughters. So that if death is necessary, then the means in that respect are as necessary. Which to the end you may the better perceive by examples, I will not refuse in conceit and imagination to wander a while with you through the great university of the world.'

Chapter 16

Examples of necessary alteration, or death in the whole world.
That heaven and the elements are changed, and will perish; the
like is to be seen in towns, provinces, and kingdoms; finally, that
all things here do turn about the wheel, and that nothing is stable
or constant.

'It is an eternal decree, pronounced of the world from the beginning, and of all things therein, to be born and to die, to begin and to end. That supreme judge of all things would have nothing firm and stable but himself alone, as says the tragic poet:

> From age and death God only stands free,
> But all things else by time consumed be.[52]

All these things which you behold and admire either will perish in their due time, or at least be altered and changed. Do you see the sun? He faints. The moon? She labours and languishes. The stars? They fail and fall. And however the wit of man cloaks and excuses these matters, yet there have happened and daily do in the celestial body such things as confound both the rules and wits of the mathematicians. I omit comets strange in form, situation, and motion, which all the universities shall never persuade me to be in the air, or of the air. But behold our astrologers were sorely troubled of late with strange motions and new stars. This very year there arose a star whose increasing and decreasing was plainly marked,[53] and we saw (a matter hardly to be credited) even in the heaven itself, a thing to have beginning and end again. And Varro (in Augustine) cries out and affirms that "the evening star called of Plautus Versperugo and of Homer Hersperus had changed his colour, his bigness, his fashion, and his course".[54] Next to the heaven, behold the air, it is altered daily and passes into winds, clouds, and showers. Go to the waters. Those floods and fountains which we affirm to be perpetual, do sometimes fail altogether, and other times change their channel and ordinary course. The huge ocean, a great and secret part of nature, is ever tossed and tumbled with tempests; and if you are left wanting, yet it has its flowing and ebbing of waters,

and that we may perceive it to be subject to decay, it swells and
swages daily in its parts.

Behold also the earth which is taken to be immovable, and to stand
steady of its own force: it faints and is stricken with an inward secret
blast that makes it tremble. Somewhere it is corrupted by the water,
elsewhere by fire. For these same things do strive among themselves.
Neither grudge you to see war among men, there is likewise between
the elements. What great lands have been wasted, even wholly
swallowed up by the sudden deluges and violent overflowings of the
sea? In old times the sea overwhelmed wholly a great island called
Atlantis (I think not the story fabulous) and after that the mighty cities
Helice and Bura. But to leave ancient examples, in our own father's
age here in Belgica two islands with the towns and men in them. And
even now in our time this lord of the sea, Neptune, opens to himself
new gaps and sweeps up daily the weak banks of Frizeland and other
countries. Yet does not the earth sit still like a slothful housewife, but
sometimes revenges herself and makes new islands in the midst of
the sea, though Neptune marvel and be moved at that. And if these
great bodies which to us seem everlasting be subject to mutability
and alteration, why much more should not towns, commonwealths,
and kingdoms, which must needs be mortal, as they that do compose
them? As each particular man has his youth, his strength, old age, and
death, so fares it with those other bodies. They begin, they increase,
they stand and flourish, and all to this end, that they may decay. One
earthquake under the reign of Tiberius overthrew twelve famous
towns of Asia, and as many in Campania in Constantine's time. One
war of Attila, a Scythian prince, destroyed over a hundred cities.[55] The
ancient Thebes of Egypt is scarce held in remembrance in this day,
and a hundred towns of Crete not believed ever to have been. To come
to more certainty, our elders saw the ruins of Carthage, Numantia,
Corinth, and wondered at them. And we ourselves have beheld the
unworthy relics of Athens, Sparta, and many renowned cities, and
even that Lady of all things and countries, falsely termed everlasting,[56]
where is she? Overwhelmed, pulled down, burned, overflowed. She is
perished with more than one kind of destruction, and at this day she
is ambitiously sought for, but not found in her proper soil. Do you
see that noble Byzantium being proud with the seat of two Empires?
Venice lifted up with the stability of a thousand years continuance?

Their day shall come at length. And also our Antwerp, the beauty of cities, in time shall come to nothing. For this great master builder pulls down, sets up, and, if I may so lawfully speak, makes a sport of human affairs. And like an image maker, forms and frames to himself sundry sorts of portraitures in his clay.

I have spoken of towns and cities; countries likewise and kingdoms run the very same race. Once the East flourished; Assyria, Egypt, and Judea excelled in war and peace. That glory was transferred into Europe, which now, like a diseased body, seems to me to be shaken and to have a feeling of her great confusion at hand. And that which is more, and never enough, to be marvelled at, this world having now been inhabited these five thousand and five hundred years has, at last, come to its dotage. And now we may approve again the fables of Anaxarchus,[57] in old times hissed at, behold now there arises elsewhere new people, and a new world. O the law of necessity, wonderful, and not to be comprehended. All things run into this fatal whirlpool of ebbing and flowing. And some things in this world are long lasting but not everlasting.

Lift up your eyes and look about with me, for it grieves me not to stand long upon this point, and behold the alterations of all human affairs, and the swelling and swaging of them as of the sea. Arise you, fall you, rule you, obey you, hide your head; lift yours up, and let this wheel of changeable things run round, so long as this round world remains. Have you Germans in times past been fierce? You are now milder than most people of Europe. Have you British been uncivil before? Now you exceed the Egyptians and people of Sybaris in delights and riches. Has Greece once flourished? Now let her be afflicted. Has Italy swayed the sceptre? Now let her be in subjection. You Goths, you Vandals, you vilest of the barbarians, peep out of your lurking holes, and come rule the nations in your turn. Draw near you rude Scythians, and with a mighty hand hold awhile the reins of Asia and Europe; yet you again soon after give place and yield up the sceptre to another nation bordering on the ocean. Am I deceived? Or else do I see the sun of another new empire arising in the West?'

Chapter 17

We come to that necessity which is of Destiny. First Destiny itself affirmed. That there has been a general consent of the common people and wise men; but different in part. How many ways Destiny has been taken among the ancients.

Thus spoke Langius, and with his talk caused the tears to trickle down my cheeks, so clearly he seemed to behold the vanity of human affairs. With that, lifting up my voice, 'Alas', I said, 'what are we, or all these matters for which we thus toil? "What is it to be somebody? What is it to be nobody? Man is a shadow and a dream", as says the poet.'[58] Then Langius spoke to me: 'But you, young man, do not only contemplate on these things, but despise them. Imprint Constancy in your mind amid this casual and inconstant variableness of all things. I call it inconstant in respect of our understanding and judgement; for that if you look to God and his providence, all things succeed in a steady and immovable order. Now I cast aside my sword and come to my engines; neither will I any longer assault your sorrow with handy weapons but with great ordnance, running against it with the strong and terrible ram which no power of man is able to put back nor policy to prevent. This place is somewhat slippery, yet I will enter into it, but warily, slowly, and, as the Greeks say, "with a quiet foot".[59]

And first, that there is a kind of fatal destiny in things, I think neither yourself, Lipsius, nor any people or age has ever doubted of.' Here, I interrupting him, said, 'I pray you pardon me if I hinder you a little in this course. What? Do you oppose Destiny to me? Alas, this is but a weak engine pushed on by the feeble Stoics. I tell you plainly I care not a rush for the destinies nor the ladies of them.[60] And I say with the soldier in Plautus, I will scatter this troupe of old wives with one blast of breath, even as the wind does the leaves.'[61] Langius, looking sternly on me: 'Will you so rashly and unadvisedly', he said, 'delude or deny utterly Destiny? You are not able, except you can at once take away the divine Godhead and its power. For, if there is a God, there is also Providence; if it, a decree and order of things, and of that follows a firm and sure necessity of events. How do you avoid this blow? Or with what axe will you cut off this chain?

For God and that eternal spirit may not otherwise be considered by us, than that we attribute to it an eternal knowledge and foresight. We must acknowledge him to be stayed, resolute, and immutable, always one, and like himself, not wavering or varying in those things which once he willed and foresaw. For, "the eternal God never changes his mind", says Homer.[62] Which if you confess to be true, as needs you must, if there be in you any reason or sense, it also must be allowed that all God's decrees are firm and immovable even from everlasting to all eternity; of this grows Necessity, and that same Destiny which you deride. The truth of it is so clear and commonly received, that there was never any opinion more current among all nations. And whoever had any light of God himself and his providence, had the like of Destiny. The most ancient and wisest poet Homer, believe me, traced his divine muse in none other path than this of Destiny. Neither did the other poets, his progeny, stray from the steps of their father. See Euripides, Sophocles, Pindar, and among the Latins, Virgil. Shall I speak of historiographers? This is the voice of them all: that such and such a thing came to pass by Destiny, and that by Destiny kingdoms are either established or subverted. Would you hear the philosophers, whose chief care was to find out and defend the truth against the common people? As they jarred in many things through an ambitious desire of disputing, so it is a wonder to see how they agreed universally upon the entrance into this way which leads to Destiny. I say in the entrance of that way because I do not deny that they followed many pathways, which may be reduced to these four kinds of Destiny, namely, mathematical, natural, violent, and true.[63] All of which I will expound briefly, only touching on them a little, because that from these commonly grows confusion and error.'

Chapter 18

The first three kinds of Destiny briefly explained. The definition or description of them all. The Stoics slightly and briefly excused.

'I call mathematical Destiny that which ties and knits firmly all actions and events to the power of the planets and dispositions of the stars, of which the Chaldeans and astrologists were the first authors. And among the philosophers that lofty Mercurius is principal and abettor, who subtly and wisely distinguishing Providence, Necessity, and Destiny, says, "Providence is an absolute and perfect knowledge of the celestial God, which has two faculties nearly allied to it, Necessity and Destiny. Destiny truly serves and assists Providence, and also Necessity, but to Destiny itself the stars do minister. For neither may any man avoid the force of Fate, nor beware of the power and influence of the stars. For these be the weapons and armour of Destiny, at whose pleasure they do and perform all things to nature and men".[64] In this foolish opinion are not only the common crew of astrologers, but, I shame to speak it, some divines.

    I call natural Fate the order of natural causes, which, not being hindered, by their force and nature do produce a certain and the self same effect. Aristotle is of this sect, if we give credit to Alexander of Aphrodisias his interpreter.[65] Likewise, Theophrastus, who writes plainly, "that destiny is the nature of each thing".[66] By their opinion it is destiny that a man begets a man; and so that if he dies of inward natural causes and not by violence or force, it is destiny. Contrarily, that a man should engender a serpent or a monster, is besides destiny; also to be killed with a sword or by fire. This opinion is not very offensive, for that indeed it ascends not so high as the force of Fate or Destiny. And does not every one escape falling who keeps himself from climbing aloft? Such a one is Aristotle almost everywhere writing ought of celestial matters, except in his book *On the World*, which is a golden treatise, savouring of a more celestial air.[67] I read moreover in a Greek writer that Aristotle thought that "Fate was no cause, but that chance was in some sort an alteration or change of the cause of such things as were disposed by Necessity".[68] O the heart of a philosopher, that dares to account Fortune and Chance among the number of causes, but not Destiny. But let him pass. I come to the Stoics my friends (for I profess to hold that sect in estimation and account) who were the authors of violent Fate, which with Seneca I define to be "necessity of all things and actions, which no force can withstand or break";[69] and with Chrysippus, "spiritual power, governing orderly the whole world".[70] These definitions swerve not far from the truth if they be soundly and modestly expounded. Neither, happily, do their opinions generally, if the common people had not condemned the same already by a prejudicial conceit. They are charged with two impieties, that they make God subject to the wheel of Destiny, and also the actions of our will. I cannot boldly acquit them of both these faults, for out of some of their writings (few being at this day extant) we may gather those sayings, and out of some other we collect more wholesome sentences.

Seneca, a principal pillar of that sect, stumbles at the first block of his book *On Providence* where he says, "the very same necessity binds God, an irrevocable course carries away both human and divine things. The maker and ruler of all things decreed destinies, but now follows them. He commanded once, but he obeys forever,"[71] And that same indissoluble chain and linking together of causes which binds all things and persons seems plainly to infer force or constraint. But the true Stoics never professed such a doctrine, and if by chance any like sentence passed from them in the vehemency of their writing or disputing, it was more in words than in substance and sense. Chrysippus, who first corrupted that grave sect of philosophers with crabbed subtleties of questions, clears it from depriving man of free liberty.[72] And our Seneca does not make God subject to fate (he was wiser than that) but God to God, after a certain kind of speech. For those Stoics that came nearest the truth do call Destiny sometimes Providence and sometimes God. Therefore Zeno, when he had called "Destiny a power moving about the same matter, after one and the same manner", he adds, "which it matters not whether you call it Providence or nature".[73] Likewise Chrysippus elsewhere called "Destiny the eternal purpose or decree of providence".[74] Panaetius the Stoic said, "that God himself was Fate".[75] Seneca being of the same mind says, "when you list you may call the author of nature and all things by this or that name. You may justly term him the best and great Jupiter and thundering and Stator, that is, stable or standing, not so called as historians deliver because that after a vow undertaken, he stopped the Roman army flying away, but because all things stand by his free benefit, therefore was he named stander or stabiliser. If you call him also Fate (or Destiny), you shall not lie about him. For since Destiny is nothing but a folded order of causes, he is the principal and first cause of all upon which the residue do depend".[76] Which last words are so godly spoken that slander itself cannot slander them. In this point dissented not from the Stoics, that great writer to a great king:[77] "I think that Necessity ought not to be called anything else but God, as a steadfast and stable nature. And destiny that which knits together all things and holds his course freely, without let or impediment."[78] Which sayings, if they have any taste of temerity in them, yet not impiety, and being rightly interpreted, differ not much from our true fate and destiny. I do in good earnest give this commendation to the Stoics, that no other sect of philosophers avowed more the majesty and providence of God, nor drew men nearer to heaven and eternal things. And if in treading this trace of Destiny they went somewhat astray, it was through a laudable and good desire they have to withdraw blind men from the blind Goddess, I mean Fortune, the nature of which they did not only mightily hiss out of their company, but even the very name.'

Chapter 19

The fourth and true kind of Destiny expounded. The name briefly spoken of, it is lightly defined, and proved to differ from Providence.

'This much may suffice touching the opinions and dissensions of the ancients. For why should I overcuriously "search the secrets of hell"[79] (as the proverb is)? I shall have enough to do with true Destiny, which now I propound and illustrate, calling it an eternal decree of God's providence, which cannot be taken away no more than Providence itself. And let not any man argue with me about the name, because I say there is not in Latin another proper word to express that thing but *fatum*. What? Have old writers abused it? Let us use it, and so enlarging this word out of the prison of the Stoics, let us bring it to a better light. It is called in Latin *fatum*, a *fando* of speaking,[80] neither is it anything else properly but the "saying and commandment of God". And this is it which now I seek for; I define it either with that famous Pico, "a rank and order of causes depending upon God's counsel",[81] or with my own words more obscurely and subtly, "an immovable decree of Providence inherent in things movable, which firmly effects everything in its order, place, and time". I call it "a decree of Providence" because I agree not wholly with the divines of our days (let them give me leave in the free study of the truth) who in name and nature confound it with Providence. I know it be a hard matter, and full of temerity to conceive or restrain in certain words that supernatural and supercelestial essence (I mean God) or all that belongs to him; yet to man's capacity I defend and maintain that Providence is one thing properly, and the same which we call Fate or Destiny another. For I consider Providence no otherwise than that it be a power and faculty in God of seeing, knowing, and governing all things. A power, I say, universal, undivided, guarded, and as Lucretius speaks, united together. But Destiny seems to descend into the things themselves and to be seen in the particulars of them, being as it were a disposing and bestowing abroad of that universal Providence, by particulars. Therefore Providence is in God, and attributed to him alone; destiny in the things, and is to them ascribed. You think I trifle and, as it is said, "bore holes in millet seed".[82] No, Lipsius, I take this out of the talk of the common people, among whom nothing is more usual than to say, 'this was my good or evil destiny'; and likewise, "this was the fatal decree of this kingdom, or that town". But no man speaks so of Providence, no man applies it to the things themselves without impiety and derision. Therefore, I said well, that the one of them was in God, the other truly from God, and perceived in the things themselves.

I say, moreover, that though Providence is not really divided from Destiny, yet it is more excellent and more ancient; even as we are taught in the schools of the wise to say that the sun is more worthy than the light, eternity than time, understanding than reason. But to draw into a short summary these curious and uncommon matters, you see I have just cause both to use this distinction and also to retain the name of Destiny against the new Senate of theologians. For why? Those ancient celebrated Fathers prohibit me not but that I may use in its right and true sense the word Destiny.[83] But now that I may return to make plain my former definition, I said it was "an inherent decree" to show that Destiny should be marked in the things to which it comes, and not from whence it proceeds. I added, "in movable things", signifying that although Destiny itself be immovable, yet it takes not away motion, nor any natural faculty from things, but works easily and without force even as the marks and signs imprinted by God in each thing do require. In causes (secondary, I mean) that be necessary, it works necessarily; in natural causes, naturally; in voluntary causes, voluntarily; in contingent, contingently. Wherefore in respect of the things it does neither force, nor constrain; but as everything is made to do, or suffer, so it directs and turns all things. But if you recall it to its first original, I mean God and his providence, I affirm constantly and boldly that all things are done necessarily, which are done by destiny.

Lastly, I joined the "order, place, and time", establishing that which I said before, that Providence was of things in universality, Destiny by distribution in particularities. By "order", I understand the course and uniting together of causes which Destiny limits. By "place and time", I mean that wonderful and incomprehendable power whereby all events or actions are tied to their certain places and moments of time. It was Destiny that Tarquinius should be banished from his kingdom. So be it, but first let the adultery be committed. You see the order of the causes. It was Destiny that Caesar should be killed. So, but in the senate by the image of Pompey. You see the place. That Domitian should be murdered by his own people. Let him be murdered, but at the very hour, even the fifth, which in vain he sought to prevent.[84] Thus you see the time.'

Chapter 20

It is distinguished by four notes from Stoic Destiny. Here is shown more exactly how it does not enforce our will; and also that God is neither co-worker nor author of evil.

'How say you, young man, do you perceive this? Or must I light a clearer torch for you?' I, striking my head, 'Yes, Langius, I must have more light, or I shall never come out of this darkness. What slender kind of distinctions are these? What captious snares of questions are here? I fear treason, believe me, and suspect those mystical and doubtful words of yours as my very enemies.' Langius, laughing a little, 'Be of good courage', he said, 'here is no Hannibal. You have come into a sure castle, not fallen into any ambush. I will give you light enough. Tell me where and in what point you are so ignorant yet?' 'In that, Langius, which concerns force and necessity. For truly I cannot conceive how this Destiny that you describe differs from that of the Stoics, which when you had in words shut out at the broad gate, as I may say, in effect you let in afterwards at a postern or backdoor.' 'No, Lipsius, God forbid, for my part I do not so much as dream of any such Stoic Destiny, nor study to revive again those old wives long ago dead and buried. I propose to you such a doctrine as may stand with modesty and godliness, distinguished from the violent Fate by four marks. They make God himself subject to Destiny, and Jupiter (in Homer) though he were most willing, could not enlarge Sarpedon from his bands.[85] But we do subject destiny to God, making him a most free author and actor of things, able at his will and pleasure far to surmount and cut in sunder those linked troupes and bands of Destiny. They appoint a successive order of natural causes from all eternity; we do not make the causes always natural (for God is often the cause of wonders and miracles, besides or contrary to nature) nor eternal. For these second causes had their beginning with the world. Thirdly, they take away all contingency from things; we admit it, affirming that as often as the secondary causes are such, chance or hap may be admitted in the events and actions. Lastly, they seemed to intrude a violent force upon our will. This is far from us, who do both allow Fate or Destiny, and also join hands with liberty or freedom of will. We do so shun the deceitful blasts of fortune, and chance, that we do not dash our ship against the rocks of necessity. Is there Fate? Yes. But it is the first and principal cause, which is so far from taking away the middle and secondary causes that, ordinarily and for the most part, it works not but by them; and your will is among the number of those secondary causes, think not that God forces it or wholly takes it away. Herein is all the error and ignorance in this matter, no man considers how he ought to will that which destiny wills. And I say freely to will it. For God that created all things uses the same without any corruption of them. As the highest sphere with its motion sways about the rest,[86] yet so as it neither bars nor breaks them out of their proper motions, so God by the power of Destiny draws all things but does not take away the peculiar faculty or motion of any thing. He wishes that trees and corn should grow; so they do, without any force of their own nature. He wishes that men should use deliberation and choice;

so they do, without force, of their free will. And yet whatsoever
they were in mind to make choice of, God foresaw from all eternity.
He foresaw it, I say, not forced it; he knew it, but constrained not;
he foretold it, but not prescribed it. Why do our curious priests
stagger or stumble here? O simple creatures! I see nothing more
clear than this, except it be so that some busy wanton mind lists to
rub and exasperate itself, being infected with a contagious itching of
disputation and contention.

How can it be, they say, if God foresaw that I should sin, and
his foresight cannot be deceived, but that I do sin necessarily? Fool!
Who denies it? You sin necessarily, and yet of your own free will.
This much did God foresee, that you should sin in such sort as he
foresaw, but he saw that you should sin freely, therefore you sin
freely and necessarily. Is this plain enough? They urge further, and
say, is not God in us the author of every motion? He is the author
generally, I confess, yet the favourer of good only. Are you inclined
to virtue? He knows it and helps you. To vice? He knows that also,
and suffers you. Neither is there any fault in him. I ride a weak and
lame horse, the riding is of me, but the weakness and lameness of
him. I play upon a harp ill sounding and out of tune. In that it is out
of tune is the fault of the instrument, not of me. The earth with one
universal and the same juice nourishes all trees and fruits of which
some grow to be profitable, and some poisonable. What then? Shall
we say that this proceeds of the earth, and not rather from the nature
of the trees that do convert so good nutriment into poison? So in
this case it comes from God that you are moved. But it is of and
in yourself that you are moved to evil. Finally, to conclude of this
liberty, Destiny is as the first man that leads the round in this dance
of the world; but so as we dance our parts too, in willing or nilling,
and no further, not in doing, for there is left to man only a free will
to strive and struggle against God, and not power to perform the
same. As it is lawful for me to walk up and down in a ship and to run
about the hatches or seats, but this stirring of mine cannot hinder
the sailing of the ship, so in this fatal vessel in which we all sail, let
our wills wrangle and wrest as they list, they shall not turn her out
of her course, nor any thing hinder the same. That highest will of all
wills must hold and rule the reins, and with the turn of a hand direct
this chariot wherever it pleases.'

Chapter 21

A conclusion of the treatise of Destiny. An admonition that it is doubtful and full of danger, and must not curiously be searched. Lastly, an earnest exhortation to imprint courage in our minds through necessity.

'But why do I sail on so long in this course? I will now cast about and avoid this Charybdis, which has swallowed up so many men's wits. Here I behold how Cicero suffered shipwreck, who chose rather to deny Providence than to abate one ace of man's liberty.[87] "So while he made men free (as it is finely said by one prelate) he made them sacrilegious."[88] Damascene also sails in this gulf and extends Providence to other things but excludes it from those that are in us.[89] By whose harms, Lipsius, I being warned will keep to the shore, and not launch out too far into this deep sea. Euclides being asked many things touching God, answered fitly, "Other things I know not, but of this I am assured, that he hates curious persons".[90] Even so I think of Destiny, which must be looked to, not into, and be credited, not perfectly known. I suppose that saying of Bias, "touching God, believe that he is",[91] may better be applied to Destiny, of which I admonish you this much, that it suffices to know that it is. If you are ignorant in other things belonging to it, it is no offence. This is sufficient to our purpose (for I now return from wandering, into the right way again) that you believe Necessity to be naturally born together with public evils, and henceforth seek some solace of your sorrow. What appertains it to you to inquire curiously of the liberty or servitude of our will? Whether it be enforced or persuaded? Alas poor soul! Syracuse is sacked by the enemy, and you sit drawing circles in the dust.[92] War, tyranny, slaughter, and death hang over your head, which are things truly sent from above, and do not in any way appertain to your will or pleasure. You may fear, but not prevent; fly, but not avoid them. Arm yourself against them, and take this fatal weapon in your hand, which will not only prick but kill all these sorrows; not lighten you, but wholly unload you of them. As a nettle if you touch it softly stings, but loses its force if you handle it roughly, so this grief grows greater by applying soft mollifying plasters, but is soon cured with sharp corrasives.

Now there is nothing more forcible than Necessity, which with one assault overthrows and puts to flight all these weak troops. What do you mean sorrow? It is no boot to use you when a thing of necessity must or reason ought to come to pass. What will your complaint do? You may shake this celestial yoke, but not shake it off:

> Leave off to think that God's fatal decree,
> By your repining may altered be.[93]

There is no other refuge from Necessity but to wish that that she wills. Well was it said by an excellent wise man, "You are sure to be conqueror if you enter into no conflict but such as is in your power to overcome".[94] The combat with Necessity is not such that whosoever contends shall be overcome; what more may be marvelled at, he is already vanquished before he begins to enter the lists with it.'

Chapter 22

Some do seek a cloak for their laziness in Destiny; but that is taken away. Fate works by secondary causes, therefore they must be applied. How far it beholds us to aid our country, and how not. The end of this first conference and book.

Here Langius, pausing a little, I became the readier to speak my mind, and told him that 'If this wind blew astern thus awhile, I should think myself very near the haven. For I have now a bold resolution to follow God and obey Necessity. I think I can say with Euripides, "I had rather do sacrifice to him, than incensed with ire to kick against the pricks, or that I being a mortal man should contend with God immortal".[95] Yet there is one tempestuous wave of a troubled imagination that tosses me; stop it, Langius, if you may. For if all public evils come by Destiny, which cannot be constrained nor controlled, why then shall we take any care at all for our country? Why do we not leave all to that great masterless Lord, and sit still ourselves with our hands in our bosoms?[96] For you say that all advice and aid is of no force, if Destiny be against it.' Langius replying, 'Alas, young man', he said, 'by wilful obstinacy you err from the truth. Is this the way to obey Destiny; and not rather to resist and despise it? You will sit still with your hands in your bosom. Well, I wish your tongue had been tied now. Who told you that Destiny works alone without auxiliary and mean causes?[97] It is destiny that you should have children, yet first you must sow the seed in your wife's garden; to be cured of your disease, but so as you use the physician and good nourishment.[98] So likewise if it is destiny that this weather-beaten ship of your country shall be saved from drowning, it is destiny also that she be aided and defended. If you will attain to the haven you must ply the oars, and hoist your sails, and not idly expect wind at will from heaven.

Contrarily, if it is destiny that your country shall be brought to confusion, such things shall come to pass by destiny as will bring her to desolation by human means. The princes and people shall be at variance among themselves; none shall be willing to obey; none able to command; all shall speak proudly and act cowardly. Finally, the chieftains themselves shall have neither counsel nor fidelity. Velleius said truly, "the force of fates is inevitable, whose estate they determine to confound his counsels they corrupt";[99] and again, "the matter is so that God when he will change a man's good estate takes away his understanding. And (which is most wretched of all) he causes that the misery which befalls is reputed to happen most deservedly".[100] Yet you must not be driven so into despair, as though at the first assault your country were in hazard of utter destruction. How do you know that? What can you tell whether this be only a light fit of fever, or a deeper disease to death? Therefore put to your helping hand and, as the proverb says, hope still while breath is in the sick body. But if you see by certain and infallible tokens that the fatal alteration of the State has come, with me this saying shall prevail, "not to fight against God".[101] And in such a case I would allege the example of Solon; for when Pisistratus had brought the city of Athens under his obedience, Solon, seeing that all his labour for the defence of the common liberty was in vain, came and laid down his sword and target before the Senate doors, crying out, "O my country, I have by word and deed defended you while I could".[102] And so going home he was quiet afterwards. So do you; yield to God, and give place to the time. And if you are a good citizen or commonwealth's man, preserve yourself to a better and happier end. The liberty which now is lost may be recovered again hereafter; and your decayed country may flourish in another age; why do you lose all courage and fall into despair? Of those two consuls at the battle of Cannae, I account Varro a more excellent citizen who escaped than Paulus that was slain; and so did the Senate and people of Rome judge, giving him thanks publicly for that he had not lost all hope, nor despaired wholly of the commonwealth.[103] Whether she shake or fall, whether she impair or wholly perish, do not be afflicted, but take to you the noble courage of Crates, who, when Alexander asked whether he would have his country restored again to liberty; "why should I?" said he, "for it may be that another Alexander will oppress her".[104] This is the property of wise and valiant hearted men, as Achilles warned in Homer:

> Though cause of grief be great, yet let us keep
> All to ourselves; it boots not to weep.[105]

Else as Creon (mentioned in fables) embracing his daughter while burning, did not help her, but killed himself as well;[106] so, Lipsius, you shall sooner with your tears quench the light of your own life than this general flame of your country.'

While Langius was thus speaking, the doors racked with a great noise, and behold there came a lad directly towards us, sent from that worthy personage Torrentius, to put us in mind of the hour of supper. Then Langius, as if awakening suddenly out of a sound sleep, 'Oh', he said, 'how has this talking beguiled me? How is this day stolen away?' And then he rose, taking me by the hand, and said, 'Come, Lipsius, let us go to our supper long wished for'. 'No', I said, 'let us sit still a while longer. I account this the best supper of all others, which I may call as the Greeks do, "he meat of the gods".[107] While we are at this banquet, I do always hunger, and am never satisfied'. But Langius drew me along with him, saying, 'Let us now have regard to our promise made, and that which is behind of our duty to Constancy, we will, if it please you, perform tomorrow'.

BOOK TWO

Chapter 1

*The occasion of renewing their talk. The going to Langius'
pleasant garden, and the commendation thereof.*

The next day it seemed good to Langius to bring me to his gardens,
being two, which he kept with very great care; one on the hill over
against his house, the other further off in a valley by the river of
Moze.

> Which river holds his course gently,
> By a town seated most pleasantly.[108]

Therefore coming somewhat timely into my chamber, 'What,
Lipsius', he said, 'shall we walk abroad, or had you rather take your
ease and sit still?' 'No, Langius, I would rather walk with you. But
where shall we go?' 'If it pleases you', said Langius, 'to my garden
by the river's side; the way is not far, you shall exercise your body
and see the town. Finally, the air is there pleasant and fresh in this
hot weather.' 'It pleases me well, I said, 'neither shall it in any way
be tedious for me to follow if you go before, even if it were to the
furthest Indies.' And with that, calling for our cloaks, we put them
on; we went, and went into the garden. In the very entrance as I cast
my eyes about with a wandering curiosity, wondering with myself
at the elegance and beauty of the place; 'My sire', I said, 'what
pleasantness and bravery is this? You have heaven here, Langius,
and no garden. Neither do the glittering stars above shine clearer
in a fair night than your fine flowers glistening and showing their
colours with variety. Poets speak much of the gardens of Adonis
and Alcinous; they are trifles and in comparison with this no better
than pictures of flies.' When I drew nearer and applied some of the

flowers to my nose and eyes, 'What shall I wish first', I said, 'to be all eye with Argus or nose with Catullus? This delight so tickles and feeds both my senses at once. Away, away all you odours of Arabia, you are loathsome to me in comparison with this pure and celestial air that I savour.' Then spoke Langius, wringing me softly by the hand and not without laughter: 'It is well commended of you, Lipsius, but truly neither I nor my country dame Flora, here present, do deserve these lofty and friendly praises.' 'Yes, but they are truly deserved, Langius. Do you think that I flatter you? I speak in good earnest and from my heart. The Elysian fields are not Elysian in comparison with this your farm. For behold, what exquisite neatness is here on every side? What order? How proportionally are all things disposed in their borders and places, that even checkerwork in tables is not more curious? Again, what plenty is here of flowers and herbs? What strangeness and novelty? In so much that nature seems to have compacted with in this little plot, whatsoever thing of price is comprised in this, or that new world.'

Chapter 2

The praise of gardens in general. That the care of them is ancient and from nature itself. That it was used by kings and great personages. Finally, the pleasure of them laid open before our eyes; and my wish not ungodly.

'And surely, Langius, this your industrious care of gardens is a labour well-beseeming and praiseworthy. A labour in which (if I guess not amiss) every good man as he is most temperately given, so is he drawn by nature and addicted to it. An argument of which is this, that you cannot name any kind of delight which the chief men of all ages have more affected than this. Look into the holy Scripture, and you shall see that gardens had their beginnings with the world, God himself appointing the first man his habitation therein, as the seat of a blessed and happy life. In profane writers the gardens of Adonis, of Alcinous, Tantalus, and the Hesperides are grown into fables and common proverbs. Also in very good approved histories you shall find that king Cyrus had gardens and orchards planted with his own hands; that Semiramis had goodly flowers hanging in the air; Marsinissa strange and famous garnished gardens, to the wonder of Africa. Moreover, among the ancient Greeks and Romans, how many could I allege that have cast aside all other cares and betaken themselves wholly to this study? And they are all (in a word) philosophers and wise men, who eschewing the cities and troublesome assemblies of people, contained themselves within the bounds and limits of their gardens. And among these, I think I see king Tarquinius in the time of that first old Rome, walking pleasantly in his garden, and cropping the tops of poppy. I remember Cato Censorinus given to the pleasure of gardens and writing seriously of that argument; Lucullus after his victories obtained in Asia, taking his recreation in his gardens; Sulla, who forsaking the dictatorship spent his old age joyously here; lastly I may not forget Diocletian the emperor that preferred his pot herbs and lettuce of a poor farm at Salona before the imperial sceptre and robes of purple. Neither have the common people dissented from the judgement of the better sort in this point, in that I know all honest minds and free from ambition have ever been delighted in this exercise. For there is in us a secret and natural force (the causes of which I cannot easily comprehend) which draws us to this harmless and liberal recreation, not only those that are prone by nature that way, but also such austere and grave personages as would seem to despise and deride it.

And as it is not possible for any man to contemplate heaven and those immortal spirits there without fear and reverence, so can we not behold the earth and her sacred treasures, nor the excellent beauty of this inferior world, without an inward tickling and delight of the senses. Ask your mind and understanding, it will confess itself to be led and fed with this aspect and sight. Ask your senses of seeing and smelling, they will acknowledge that they take not greater delight in anything than in the decent borders and beds of gardens. Pause for a little while and behold the multitude of flowers with their daily increasings, one in the stalk, one in the bud, another in the blossom. Mark how one fades suddenly and another springs. Finally, observe in one kind of flower the beauty, the form, the shape or fashion either agreeing or disagreeing among themselves a thousand ways. What mind is so stern that amid all these it will not bend itself with some mild thought, and be mollified thereby? Now come here awhile curious eye, and be fixed a little upon these gay and neat colours; mark well this natural purple, that sanguine, this ivory, that snowing colour; this fiery, that golden hue; and so many other colours besides, as the best painter may emulate but never be able to imitate with his pencil. Lastly, what a sweet odour is there? What piercing savour? And I know not what part of the heavenly air infused from above that it is not without cause why the poets told that flowers for the most part sprang up first from the juice and blood of their gods. O the true fountain of joy and sweet delight! O the seat of Venus and the Graces. I wish to rest myself and lead my whole life in your bowers. God grant me leave (far from all the tumults of towns) to walk with a gladsome and wandering eye amid these herbs and flowers of the known and unknown world, and to reach my hands and to cast my eyes one while to this full-grown flower, and another while to that newly in the blossom, so that my mind being beguiled with a kind of wandering retchlessness I may cast off the remembrance of all cares and troubles.'

Chapter 3

Here is argued against some curious persons that do abuse gardens to vanity and slothfulness. What is the true use of them; that they are fit for wise men and learned; and that wisdom herself was first bred and brought up in them.

When I had thus spoken sharply in voice and countenance, then Langius spoke softly to me; 'I see, Lipsius, I see you love this flourishing purple nymph, but I fear you dote upon her. You commend gardens but so as you seem only to admire vain and outward things therein, neglecting the true and lawful delights of them. You look only upon colours and borders, and are greedy of strange flowers brought from all parts of the world. And to what end is all this? Except it be that I might account you one of that sect, which is risen up in our days, of curious and idle persons who have made a thing that was in itself good and without offence to be the instrument of two foul vices, vanity and slothfulness. For even to this end they have their gardens; they do vaingloriously hunt after strange herbs and flowers, which having got, they preserve and cherish more carefully than any mother does her child; these are the men whose letters fly abroad into Thracia, Greece, and India only for a little root or seed. These men will be more grieved for the loss of a newfound flower than of an old friend. Would not any man laugh at that Roman which mourned in black for the death of a fish that he had.[109] So do these men for a plant.

Now if any of these whom you see come here to my dame Flora for flowers, happen to get any new or strange one, how does he boast of it? His companions do grudge and envy at him, and some of them return home with a heavier heart than ever did Sulla or Marcellus when they were put back in their suit for the praetorship. What should I call this but a kind of merry madness, not unlike the striving of children about their little puppets and dolls?

Yet consider moreover what great pains they take in these gardens. They sit, walk about the alleys, stretch themselves like sluggards, and sleep, so as they make that place not only a nursery of idleness but a very monument to their slothfulness. A profane generation of men, whom I may rightly banish from the ceremonies and communion of true gardens which I know were ordained for modest recreation, not for vanity; for solace not for sloth. What? Shall I be so light-headed as to be lifted up or pressed down in mind for the getting or losing of some rare and strange herb? No, rather I will esteem all things according to their worth, and setting aside the enticement of rareness and novelty, I know they are but herbs or flowers; that is, things fading and of small consequence. Of which the poet speaks very fitly "that Zephirus with his blast brought up some and withered others".[110] Therefore I do not despise the beauty and elegance of them (as you may see for example here before your eyes), but I dissent from the opinion of these great garden masters, in that I get them without much travel, keep them without care, and lose them without grief. Again I am not so simple or base-minded as to tie or wed myself to the shadows of my garden. I find some business even in the midst of my idleness; my mind is there busied, without any labour, and exercised without pain. "I am never less solitary (said one) than when I am alone; nor never less idle than when I am at leisure".[111] A worthy saying, which I dare swear had its first beginning in these self same gardens that I speak of. For they be ordained not for the body but for the mind, and to recreate it, not to besot it with idleness, only as a wholesome withdrawing place from the cares and troubles of this world. Are you weary of the concourse of people? Here you may be alone. Has their worldly business tired you? Here you may be refreshed again, where the food of quietness and gentle blowing of the pure and wholesome air will even breathe a new life into you. Do you consider the wise men of old times? They had their dwelling in gardens. The studious and learned wits of our age? They delight in gardens; and in them (for the most part) are compiled those divine writings of theirs which we wonder at, and which no posterity or continuance of time shall be able to abolish. So many sharp and subtle disputations of natural philosophy proceed from those green bowers. So many precepts of manners from those shadowy Academies. Out of the walks and pleasant aisles of gardens spring those sweet abounding rivers which with their fruitful overflowings have watered the whole world. For why? The mind lifts up and advances itself more to these high thoughts when it is at liberty to behold its own home, heaven, than when it is enclosed within the prisons of houses or towns. Here you learned poets compose some poems worthy of immortality. Here let all the learned meditate and write; here let the philosophers argue and dispute of contentation, constancy, life, and death. Behold, Lipsius, the true end and use of gardens, to wit, quietness, withdrawing from the world, meditation, reading, writing, and all this as it were by way of recreation and sport. As painters having dimmed their eyes with long and earnest beholding their work do recomfort them with certain glasses or green colours, so here may we refresh our wearied and wandering minds.

And why should I conceal my intent from you? Do you see that arbour curiously wrought with sundry pictures cut out of the green boughs? The same is the house of my muses, my nursery and school of wisdom. Here I either ply myself with diligent and earnest reading, or else sow in my heart some seed of good thoughts, and thereby lay up some wholesome lessons in my mind, as it were weapons in an armoury, which are always ready with me at hand against the force and mutability of fortune. So soon as I put my foot within that place, I bid all vile and servile cares abandon me, and lifting up my head as upright as I may, I despise the delights of the profane people, and the great vanity of human affairs. I seem to shake off everything in me that is human, and to be rapt up on high upon the fiery chariot of wisdom. Do you think when I am there that I take any care what the Frenchmen or Spaniards are practising, who possess the sceptre of Belgica or who is deprived of it? Whether the tyrant of Asia threatens us by sea or by land? Or finally "what the king of the cold country under the north pole imagines"?[112] No, none of all these things trouble my brain. I am guarded and fenced against all external things and settled within myself, careless of all cares save one, which is that I may bring in subjection this broken and distressed mind of mine to Right Reason and God, and subdue all human and earthly things to my mind. That whenever my fatal day shall come, I may be ready with a good courage joyfully to welcome it, and depart this life not as thrust out at the window but as let out at the door. This is my recreation, Lipsius, in my gardens. These are the fruits which I will not exchange, so long as I am in my right mind, for all the treasure of Persia and India.'

Chapter 4

An exhortation therefore to wisdom. By it we come to Constancy. Young men are seriously admonished to join the grave study of philosophy with those other studies that are more pleasant and plausible.

Thus Langius made an end of speaking, and with his last profound and constant talk, I confess he made me amazed. Yet recalling myself, 'O happy man', I said, 'both in tranquillity and troubles! O more than manly courage in a man! I wish to God I were able in some measure to imitate, and to creep after your footsteps, as though I came far behind.' Here Langius, reprehending me, 'What talk you of imitating? You may easily exceed me, and not only follow, but far pass me. For I myself, Lipsius, have trod but very little in this path of Constancy and Virtue. Neither am I to be compared as yet to the valiant and good men, but perchance am a little better than the most effeminate and worst sort. But you, whose disposition is lusty and quick, set yourself forwards and under my conduct enter into this highway which leads directly to stability and Constancy. The way that I speak of is wisdom, whose even and easy track I pray and admonish you that you do not cease to tread. Have you delighted in learning and the company of those nine sisters?[113] I like it well, knowing that by this lighter and pleasant kind of learning, the mind is prepared and made ready "not being fit before to receive the sacred seed".[114] How is it I allow not that you should stay there and make that both the beginning and perfection of all your studies? These must be the foundation, not the work itself. The way to the mark, but not the goal or mark itself that we run at. If you were bidden to a banquet I believe you would not only taste of marzipans and junkets, but first settle your stomach with some stronger meat; why should not the same be done in this public feast of learning? Why, I say, join we not to the firm food of philosophy, with the sweet delicates of orators and poets? Mistake me not, I do not condemn these latter but commend them in their place; and I would have those loose wandering nymphs to be bridled, as I may say, by some severe Bacchus.

The wooers that Homer writes of are worthily scoffed, who, missing Penelope, became suitors to her maids.[115] Beware you do not likewise and, forsaking the lady of all, fall in love with her servants. It is a plausible kind of praise to be called a learned man, but better to be called a wise man, and best of all to have the title of a good man. Let us follow this, and by many labours let us not covet to know alone but to be wise and do thereafter:

> How little worth is learning's skill,
> Where wisdom is not present still?[116]

So says the old verse truly. How many are there at this day of the festival of the Muses that do disgrace both themselves and the name of learning? Some, for that they are replenished with vices and wickedness; many for that they be vain, inconstant, only speculative, and given to no fruitful or profitable study. Even though they understand Greek and Latin authors? That is all; they do nothing but understand them. And as Anacharsis spoke prettily of the Athenians, that they used money only to cast accounts withal;[117] so these men have their knowledge to no end, but to know. So little care have they of their life and deeds, in my conceit, that it is not without cause that learning is so ill spoken of among the multitude, as if it were a mistress to ungodliness. How is it good letters being rightly used are a directory to virtue, couple wisdom with them; to which learning ought to prepare and frame our wits, not to detain or challenge them to itself. For as some trees will bear no fruit except they grow near to others that be of the male kind, no more will these tender virgins (I mean good letters), unless they be conjoined with the manly courage of wisdom.

Why do you correct the writings of Tacitus, if your own life is uncorrected?[118] Why do you illustrate Tranquillus, you yourself being in the dark mist of errors? Why are you so careful in purging Plautus from faults and imperfections, when your own mind is full of foul filth and sluttishness? Give yourself at length to better studies, and get learning that may serve you not for vain ostentation but to some good use and purpose. Apply yourself to wisdom, which may amend your evil manners, set at rest and beautify your distempered and unclean mind. She only is able to imprint virtue and to work the impression of Constancy in you, and to set open to you the temple of a good mind.'

Chapter 5

That wisdom is not obtained by wishing, but by working. A returning to the former talk of Constancy. That desire of learning is a good sign in youth.

This admonition wrought in me an earnest desire which I could not conceal; and thereupon I said, 'My father, in heart and mind I follow you, when shall I be able in deeds to do so? When will that day come when I shall be free from all these cares that trouble me, and tread the trace that leads to true wisdom, whereby I may attain to Constancy?' Langius, taking me up short, 'What? Do you betake yourself to wishing rather than doing? It is spoken fondly, and as the common sort of men uses. For it cannot be that as fables make mention how Caeneus with a wish was transformed from a woman into a man;[119] so you should of a fool be suddenly made wise, and of a light person, become constant with wishing. You must bestow your labour withal and, as the saying is, join hands with heart. Seek, read, learn.' 'I know, Langius', I said, 'that I must do so, but I pray you set too your helping hand and proceed forwards in your yesterday's talk that was interrupted by going to supper. Return again to Constancy, the ceremonies of whose honour having been begun to be celebrated, may not be discontinued without sacrilege.'

Langius shaking his head a little, 'No, Lipsius', he said, 'I will not do it, lest I shut up myself again in this schoolhouse. This is no place fit for our purpose, which you know well I made for my ease, not for my pains; we will at some other time prosecute that argument.' 'No, even now', I said, 'for what place is more fit for such wise communication than that your school of wisdom? I mean your fair summer house, which to me is, as it were, a temple, and the table therein instead of an altar, where sitting we may rightly sacrifice to this saint.[120] And again, I have a guess of good luck therehence.' 'What is that?', said Langius. 'That even as they who sit in apothecaries' shops carry with them in their clothes some savour of the place, so I have good hope that some scent of wisdom will stick in my mind by residing in her study.' Langius laughing, 'I fear me', he said, 'your conjecture is so light that it will weigh just nothing. Yet let us go there, Lipsius, for I tell you without dissimulation this honest ardent desire of yours somewhat moves and provokes me. And as they that search for water-springs, when they perceive in the morning a steam arising out of the earth, do make conjecture that waters lie there underneath, so I have great good hope of the fruitful streams of virtue when I see and behold in a young man an earnest desire of learning.' And with those words he brought me to his summer-house and into it; he set himself down at the table. I, turning to the boys that were there, 'Ho sirs', I said, 'stand you and keep watch. And first of all, lock the door. Do you hear me? If anybody comes in here to us alive, you shall be for it. I will have neither man nor dog nor woman to be let in; no, not Good Fortune herself if she comes.' Then Langius, laughing outright, said, 'Have you at any time been a Viceroy, your mandates are so majestical and severe.' 'I know', I said, 'it is necessary for me to be beware by the hard warning we had last night. Hold you on your talk in God's name.'

Chapter 6

The third argument for Constancy, taken for profit. That calamities are good for us, whether we respect their beginning or end. For the origin of them is God, who is eternally and immutably good, and therefore not the cause of any evil.

Langius not meditating long began thus: 'In the communication that I had yesterday of Constancy, I will constantly persevere, following those same methods and containing my tongue within the bounds which I before prescribed. You know that I had four bands or troops of soldiers to fight for Constancy against your sorrow and despair of courage, of which I have trained into the field the two former, which were Providence and Necessity.[121] And I proved sufficiently that public calamities were sent from God alone. Also that they were necessary and by no flying away to be avoided. Now I set forwards my third troop, under the leading of profit, in which serves the legion which I may well term aiding. A valiant and politic troop it is, if you mark it well. For I know not how it creeps softly and insinuates itself into the minds of men, and with a kind of flattering force overcomes them willingly. It steals rather than rushes upon us, entices not enforces, and we are as easily led by profit as drawn by necessity. This profit, Lipsius, I oppose against you and your weak bands.

I say these public calamities which we suffer are profitable to us accompanied with an inward fruit and commodity. Do we call them evils? No, rather they are good if we pluck aside the veil of opinions and cast our eyes to the beginning and end of them, of which the one is from God, the other for good. The origin of these miseries, as I proved plainly yesterday, is of God. That is, not only of the chief good, but also of the author, head, and fountain of all goodness, from whom it is as impossible that any evil should proceed, as it is for himself to be evil. The divine power is bountiful and healthful, refusing to do or receive harm, whose chief virtue is to do good. Therefore the ancients, though they were void of the knowledge of God, yet having some conceit of him in their brain, called him *Iuppiter a iuvando*,[122] that is, of helping. Do you imagine that he is angry, or choleric, and casts as it were those noisome darts among men? You are deceived. Anger, wrath, revenge are names of human affections; and proceeding from a natural frailty and weakness, are incident only to weaklings. But that divine spirit does still persevere in his bounty, and those same bitter pills which he ministers to us as medicines, though sharp in taste, are yet wholesome in operation. Well was it said by that prince of philosophers, "God does no evil, neither is the cause of any".[123] Better and more significantly spoke our wise master: "What is the cause that God does good? His own nature. He is deceived whoever thinks that God can or will do hurt. He can neither suffer nor do wrong. The first worship of God is to believe him. Then to attribute to him his majesty, and also his goodness without which there is no majesty, to know that it is he who is governor of the world that rules all things as his own, that takes upon him the tuition of all mankind, and more carefully, of every particular person. He neither does evil to others nor has any in himself."[124]

Chapter 7

Likewise, that the end of calamities tends always to good, albeit they are effected often by hurtful persons, and for harm's sake; but God breaks and bridles their force. And that all things are turned to our benefit. By the way is shown why God uses the instrument of wicked men in inflicting calamities.

'Therefore, these calamities are good in respect of their beginning, and likewise in regard of their end, because they are ever directed to good and safety (surely in good men). You will object and say, how can this be? Is it not evident that these wars and slaughters are committed with an intent to harm and hurt? It is true so, in respect of men, but not in respect of God. So that you may more plainly and fully conceive this, I must apply the light of a distinction. There are two sorts of calamities sent from God, some simple, some mixed. The first I call those which proceed purely from God without any interposition of man's policy or force. The second, which are of God, yet wrought by the ministry of men. Of the former kind are famine, dearth, earthquakes, openings of the earth, overflowings of waters, sickness, death. Of the latter are tyranny, war, oppression, slaughters. In those first all things are pure and without spot, as springing from a most pure fountain. In the latter I deny not that there is some filth and mixture, because they are conveyed and derived through the foul conduits of affections. Is man a means for effecting them? What marvel then is it if there be a fault and offence committed in accomplishing them? Marvel more at the provident goodness of God who converts that fault to our furtherance, and the offence to our good. Do you see a tyrant breathing out threatenings and murders, whose delight is in doing harm, who could be content to perish himself, so he may persecute others? Let him alone; he strays from his right mind. And God, as it were, by an invisible string leads him to his destruction. As an arrow comes to the mark without any feeling of him that shot it, so do these wicked ones. For that supreme power bridles and keeps under control all men's power, and directs their straying course to the happy haven. As in an army the soldiers have sundry affections, one fighting for pay, another for praise, another for hatred, yet they all in their princes quarrel and for the victory. So all men's wills, be they good or bad, fight under God, and among sundry and manifold ends, at length they come all to this end of ends, as I may say.

But you will demand why God uses the means of evil men? Why does he not inflict those grievous punishments immediately himself, or else by the ministry of good men? O man, you are too curious in enquiring; neither do I know whether it lie in my power to open these secrets to you. This I know well, that he has reason of his doings, even then when we are furthest off from perceiving any. And yet what strange or new thing is this? The president of a province commands an offender to be punished by the laws, yet the punisher is some officer or sergeant. The father of a great family sometimes corrects his son himself, other times he commands a servant or schoolmaster to do it. Why should we not grant to God so much authority as to them? Why shall not he when it pleases him scourge us with his own hand, and again when it seems good to him, by the means of others? For in this there is no wrong or injury. Is the servant that punishes you angry with you? Has he an intent to do you harm? It makes no matter, have you respect to the mind of him that commanded. For your father who required it stands by, and he will not suffer you to have one stripe more than his own appointment.

But why is sin mixed here withal, and the poison of passions
fasted to these divine darts? You drive me now to a steep mountain,
yet I will assay to climb up. God, to the end that he might show
forth his wisdom and great power, "has thought it better (the words
are Augustine's) to make good of evil, than to permit no evil at
all";[125] for what is wiser or better than he who can gather good from
those evil, and turn things to health and safety, that were devised to
destruction? We praise the physician that compounds the venomous
viper with this theriac to work a wholesome effect; why will you
control God if to these healthful dregs of calamities and afflictions
he adds some faults of men without any offence to you? For surely
he boils away and consumes to nothing that poison adjoined, with
the secret purging fire of his providence. Finally it makes for the
advancement of his power and glory, to which he refers all things
necessarily. For what is more able to express his mighty power, than
that he does not only vanquish his enemies that withstand him, but
so overrules them that he draws them to his party? That they fight
in his quarrel? And bear arms for his victory? This thing daily comes
to pass, when God's will is performed in the wicked, but not of the
wicked. When those things which ungodly men do against his will,
he turns them so that they come not to pass without his will. And
what stranger miracle can there be, "than that wicked men should
make them good, that were evil before".[126]

Behold, you Caesar shall help a little to our purpose. Go your
way and tread under foot two things religiously to be esteemed, to
wit, your country and son in law. This your ambition (unawares to
you) shall do service to God, and to your country, against which it
aspired; for it shall be the restoring and preserving of the Roman
state. You Attila, thirsting after blood and booty, hasten here from
the uttermost ends of the earth; take to you by strong hand, slay,
burn and waste. This your cruelty shall fight for God, and do
nothing else but stir up the Christians which were drowned and
buried in vain delights and pleasures. What do you do, you two
Vespasians?[127] Destroy the country of Jewry and the people; take
and sack the holy city. To what end? You verily do it for your glory
and the augmentation of your empire; but you err. You are only
the officers and sergeants of God's severe punishments upon that
ungodly nation. Go to, even you, by chance, that put the Christians

to death at Rome, revenge the death of Christ in Jewry.

And now, O you that are our president, whether it be from West or East, what do you intend by this war and bloody weapons? Even to strengthen the dignity of your kingdom, and the power of your own nation. But in vain, for even you are nothing else but a whip and a scourge of the wanton and lascivious Flemings. We know not how to concoct our great felicities without the help of these Neronian hot baths. These examples are occurrent in all ages, where we see that God, by the wicked lusts of some men, has accomplished his own good pleasure; and by the injustice of other men has executed his just judgements wherefore, Lipsius, let us admire this hidden force of his wisdom, and not aspire to know it; and let us be assured that all these great afflictions are to good end and purpose; although this blind mind of ours perceives it not, or slowly attains to the understanding thereof. For the true ends of afflictions are often hidden from us, which notwithstanding shall have their due course though to us unknown, not unlike certain rivers, which being removed from our sight, and running under the ground, are yet carried into their own sea.'

Chapter 8

It is here more distinctly spoken of the ends themselves. They are threefold. To whom every of them does agree. The somewhat more at large touching exercising, which profits good men in more ways than one: by strengthening, by proving, by giving example to others.

'But if it is lawful for me to hoist sails and carry my ship deeper into this sea of divine matters, I could happily speak somewhat of the ends themselves more plainly and more profoundly, first adding that saying of Homer, "if it lie in my power, or if the thing itself will admit the same".[128] For there are some of those ends which it seems I can well enough conceive myself and make known to others; some also there are which I perceive doubtfully and with a confused sight. Of the first kind of ends which are certain, there are these three: exercising, chastising, punishment. For if you mark it well you shall

find that these grievous afflictions sent by God do commonly either
exercise the good, chastise offenders, or punish the wicked; and all
this for our good. And to stand awhile upon explaining the first
branch, we see daily the best sort of men to be subject to calamities
either privately or else to be partakers of them with the wicked. We
mark and marvel at this because we neither sufficiently conceive
the cause, nor consider the consequence. The cause is God's love
towards us, and not hatred. The end or consequence is not our
hurt, but our benefit. For this exercising furthers us more ways than
one; it confirms or strengthens us, it tries or proves us; it makes us
mirrors of patience to others.

It does strengthen us, for that the same is, as it were, our schoolhouse in which God trains up his servants in Constancy and Virtue.
We see those that exercise the feats of wrestling or barriers endure
many hard trials, that they may get the mastery; so think that we
ought to do in this warfare of adversity. For why? That same our
trainer and master of the game is such a one as requires patience and
pains, not only to sweating but even to bleeding. Do you think that
he will handle his scholars tenderly, that he will dandle them with
delights upon his knee? No, he will not do so. Mothers for the most
part do corrupt their children, and make them wantons with tender
upbringing; but their fathers hold them in awe with more severity.
God is our father, therefore he loves us truly, yet with severity. If
you will be a mariner, you must be taught in tempests. If a soldier,
in perils. If you are a man indeed, why do you refuse afflictions,
seeing there is no other way to Constancy? Do you consider those
lither and lazy bodies upon whom the Sun seldom shines, or the
wind blows, or any sharp air breathes? Even such are the minds of
these nice folk that feel nothing but felicity, whom the least blast of
adverse fortune blows down and resolves into nought. Therefore
adversity does confirm and strengthen us. And as trees that are
much beaten with the wind take deeper root, so good men are the
better contained within the compass of virtue, being sometimes
assaulted with the storms of adversity.

They do moreover prove and try us. Else how could any man be
assured of his own proceeding and firmness in virtue? If the wind
blows always merrily astern, the pilot shall have no opportunity to
try his cunning. If all things succeed prosperously and happily to a

man, there is no place to make proof of his virtue; for the only true level to try with is affliction. Demetrius said worthily, "I account nothing more unfortunate than that man which never had feeling of adversity".[129] Very true it is. For our general does not spare such soldiers, but mistrusts them, neither does he affect and love, but disdain and despise them. I say he does dismiss them out of his company as base cowards and dastards.

Finally, they serve in place of mirrors or precedents. For that the Constancy and Patience of good men in miseries is as a clear light to this obscure world. They provoke others by their example, and tread the path in which they should walk. Bias lost both his goods and country, but his words sound in the ears of men at this day: "that they should carry all their goods about them".[130] Regulus was unworthily put to death by torments, but his worthy example of keeping his promise lives yet.[131] Papinianus was murdered by a tyrant,[132] but the same butcherly axe that cut off his head emboldens us to suffer death for justice's sake. Finally, so many notable citizens we see violently and injuriously either banished or murdered; but out of the rivers of their blood we do, as it were, drink Virtue and Constancy every day. All which things should lie hidden in dark corners of oblivion, were it not for the bright firebrands of these common afflictions and calamities. For as costly spices do give a sweet savour far off, if they are bruised, even so the fame of Virtue is spread abroad when it is pressed with adversity.'

Chapter 9

Of chastisement, which is the second end. It is proved to be for our benefit, in two manner of ways.

'Another end why God sends afflictions is for our chastisement, which I say is the best and gentlest that may be for our amendment. It helps and heals us in two manner of ways: either as a whip when we have offended; or as a bridle to hold us back from offending. As a whip, because it is our father's hand that does often scourge us when we do amiss; but it is a butcherly fist that strikes seldom, and then pays home for all at once. As fire or water are used to purge filth, so is this purgatory of persecutions to our sins. This whip, Lipsius, is now worthily bestowed upon us. We Flemings have of a long time fallen in the lapse, and being corrupted with delights and excess of wealth, we have wandered in the slippery paths of viciousness. But that great God does admonish and gently reclaim us, giving us a few stripes, that being warned thereby we may come again to ourselves, yea rather to him. He has taken from us our goods, which we abused to luxuriousness. Our liberty, which we abused licentiously. And so with this gentle correction of calamities, he does, as it were, purge and wash away our wickedness. A right gentle correction it is. For alas, what a slender satisfaction may we call it? It is said that when the Persians would punish any nobleman, they took away his garments and hood, and hanging those up, did beat them instead of the man; even so does this our father, who in all his chastisements touches not us, but our bodies, our fields, our wealth, and all external things.

Likewise chastisement serves as a bridle, which he reins fitly when he sees us running to wickedness. As physicians do sometimes upon good advice let blood, not because the party is sick but to prevent sickness, so God by these afflictions takes away something from us, which else would foster and nourish vices in us. For he knows the nature of all men who created them all. He judges not of diseases by the veins or colour, but by the very heart and innards. Does he see the Tuscan wits to be sharp and waspish? He keeps them under with a prince. Does he see the Swiss to be of disposition peaceable and quiet? He gives them liberty. The Venetians to be of a mean between both? He permits to them a mixed or mean kind of government. All which peradventure he will change in time, if those people alter their dispositions. Yet notwithstanding we murmur, saying, "Why are we longer afflicted with war than others?" Or "why are we held in more cruel bondage?" O fool, and sick at the very heart! Are you wiser than God? Tell me, why does the physician administer to one patient more wormwood or lingwort than to another? Because the disease or disposition of the party so requires. Even so think of yourself. He sees this people to be somewhat stubborn and therefore that they must be kept under with corrections; another nation more meek that may be brought under obedience only with shaking of the rod. But it may be that to you it seems otherwise. What makes that to the matter? Parents will not suffer knives or weapons in the hands of their child, though he weep for it, because they foresee the danger. Why should God give us too much of our will to our own destruction? Indeed we are very babes, and know not how to ask for things that are for our health, nor to avoid that which is hurtful. Notwithstanding, if need you must, weep your fill; yet you will drink of the cup of afflictions which that heavenly physician offers you full to the brim, not without good advice.'

Chapter 10

Finally that punishment itself is good and wholesome, in respect of God, of men, and of the party that is punished.

'But punishment I confess belongs to evil men, and yet is not itself evil. For first it is good we have respect for God, whose eternal and inviolable law of justice requires that men's faults be either cured or cut off. Now, chastisement reforms those that may be amended; punishment cuts away the incurable. It is good again in regard of men, among whom no society can stand or continue if busy and ungodly wits may practise what they please uncontrolled. And as it is expedient for the security of each private person to have execution done upon a particular thief or murderer, so is it necessary in general that the like justice is shown upon notorious public malefactors. These punishments upon tyrants and spoilers of the whole world must necessarily be inflicted sometimes, that they may be mirrors to admonish us, "that it is the eye of justice which beholds all things",[133] which also may cry out to other princes and people, 'learn justice now by this, and God above despise no more'.[134]

Thirdly, punishment is good in respect of those that are punished; for it is not properly vengeance or revenge, neither does the gentle deity "punish rigorously in rage", as a wicked poet said it well;[135] but it is only a prohibition and restraint from wickedness. And as the Greeks do significantly express it, "chastisement, but not revengement".[136] As death is many times sent to good men before they fall into a grievous sin, so it happens to those that act desperately wicked in the midst of their ungodliness, which they do love so much that they cannot be drawn from it except if they be clean cut off. Therefore God stops us of our unruly course, gently taking away offenders and such as are running into sin. To conclude, all punishment is good, in respect of justice; as impunity or lack of due correction is evil, which suffers men to live until they are more and more wicked, that is, miserable. Boethius spoke wittily, "the wicked that abide some punishment are happier than if no rod of justice did correct them".[137] And he yields a reason, because some good befalls them (to wit, correction), which they had not before in the catalogue of their faults.'

Chapter 11

Of the fourth end, which is uncertain to man. That it appertains either to the preservation and safety, or else to the ornament and beauty, of the whole world. Every one of these points largely handled.

'The three ends aforesaid, Lipsius, are certain and evident, which I have passed over with sure footing. The fourth remains, in which I waver, for the same is more secret and farther removed than that the capacity of man's reason can attain to it. I see it only through a cloud, and I may conceive it, but not know it; wander towards, but not to it. This end of which I speak is general, and respects either the conservation of the whole world, or the ornament of it. And touching the conservation I do therefore conjecture, because that same great God which has wisely created and ordered all these things, so made them as that he has disposed them all in "easure, number, and weight",[138] neither is it lawful for anything in its kind to surpass that mean, without the overthrow and ruin of the whole. Even so those great bodies, the heaven, the sea, and earth have their bounds. So every age has its prescribed number of living creatures. Likewise is it in men, towns, and regions: will any of these exceed their bounds? Then of necessity some whirlwind and tempest of misfortune must consume them, or else they would hurt and deface the beautiful frame of this world. But it is apparent that they do often strive to exceed their number, especially those creatures that by nature do engender and increase. Behold men, who can deny that by nature we spring up a great deal more than die? So that two men do sometimes within the space of a few years procreate a hundred out of their bodies, of whom ten or twenty do not die. Herds of cattle also would increase without number if butchers did not choose and cull out yearly certain of them for the market. Likewise birds and fishes would in a short space pester the air and the waters, were it not for fighting and war among themselves, and also deceptions practised against them by men. In every age cities and towns are built, and if burnings or other destructions happened not, our world nor scarce another would contain them. And so in concept you may pass through the nature of all things. Therefore, is it any marvel if that old father of the family thrust in his sickle into this rank field, and cut off some superfluous thousands with pestilence or war? If he did not so, what country would be able to contain us? What land could afford us nourishment? Therefore in God's name let some parts perish, that the whole perfection of all may be perpetual. For even as to governors of commonwealths the safeguard of the people is the highest law, so is the world to God.

And concerning the beauty or ornament of the world, my conjecture is twofold. First, for that I can conceive no trimness in this huge engine without a different change and variety of things. I know that the sun is most beautiful, yet the dewy night and the mantle of that black dame put between, makes it appear more gracious. The summer is most pleasant, yet the winter makes it more lovely with her icy marble and white snow. Which things if you take away, in truth you deprive us of the inward delight and feeling both of sun and summer. In this our earth, one uniform fashion pleases me not, but I take pleasure to behold the champion country and mountains, valleys and rocks, fields tilled and sea sands, meadows and woods. Satiety and loathsomeness is ever a companion of uniformity or likeness. And upon this stage of my life, why should one fashion of attire and gesture content me? No, it shall not. But, in my mind, let there be times of great quietness, and therein some naughtiness, which soon after tumults of war and the rage of cruel tyrants may take away. Who would wish this world to be like a dead sea, without wind or waves?

But I perceive moreover another kind of ornament, of more account and inward profit. Histories do teach me that all things become better and quieter after the storms of adversities. Does war vex any nation? The same does also quicken them, and most commonly bring in arts, together with other things, that do diversely adorn their wits. The Romans in times past imposed a grievous yoke upon the neck of the whole world, but yet a yoke that proved wholesome in the end, whereby barbarism was expelled from our minds, as the sun drives away darkness from our eyes. What would the Frenchmen, we ourselves, and the Germans have been at this day, if the light of that mighty empire had not shined upon us? Fierce, uncivil, delighting in slaughters between ourselves and others, despisers of God and men. Even so, I guess, it will come to pass with the new world which the Spaniards have wasted with a profitable severity, and themselves will shortly replenish again with people and inhabit it. And as they which have great nurseries for plants do remove some, set others, and cut off others, ordering them with skill for their own good and benefit; even so does God in this wide field of the world. For he is a most skilful husbandman, and at one time he breaks off some waste branches of families, another time he crops and cuts away a few leaves of particular men. This helps the stock of the tree, albeit those branches perish, and those leaves are blown away with the wind. Again he sees this nation very bare and barren of virtues; he casts it out. Another rough and unfruitful; he removes it. And some he confounds among themselves and by grafting makes, as it were, a medley of them. You Italians wax feeble and effeminate in the declining of your empire, why do you hold the best country of the world? Give place. Let the stern and sturdy Lombards manure with more happiness this soil. You wicked and wanton Greeks, perish utterly; and let those cruel Scythians be set, led, and wax wild in your country. And moreover with a certain confusion of nations you French men possess Gaul; you Saxons, Britain; you Normans seize upon Belgica and the territories bordering. All which matters, Lipsius, and many more, are manifest out of histories and by the events of things, to any diligent reader.

Therefore let us lift up ourselves, and whatsoever damage we sustain privately, let us know that it does good in some part of the whole world. The rooting out of one nation or kingdom, is the raising up of another. The decay of one tower, the building of another. And nothing properly dies or perishes here, but alters. Are we Flemings alone in account and estimation before God? Alone continually happy and Fortune's white sons? O fools! That great grandame has many more children whom we must be contented that she cherish and lull in her lap one after another, because she either cannot or will not dally with them all at once. The sun has shined with its bright beams a long time upon us. Now let it be night with us awhile, and let the glittering light illuminate the Spaniards and farthest western parts. Seneca, after his manner, says fitly and profoundly to this purpose: "A wise man should not take in ill part whatever happens to him. But let him know that those same things which seem to annoy him do belong to the preservation of the whole world, and are of the number of those things that do consummate the course and office of the whole".'[139]

Chapter 12

An old and common objection against God's justice, why punishments are not equal. Such inquiry is removed from men, and declared to be ungodly.

Here, while Langius paused a little, I spoke thus: 'As a fair water spring to travellers in summer, so is your talk to me. It cherishes, refreshes, and with a cooling kind of moisture qualifies my fever and fervent heat. But yet it qualifies, not quenches the same. There sticks a thorn in my mind (which also pricked the ancients) touching the equality of punishments. For what, Langius, is that equal balance of justice if this sword of afflictions

> Does often let wicked men go free,
> And slay such folk as good and harmless be?[140]

Why, I say, are some innocent people rooted out and the children and posterity afflicted for the faults of their ancestors? This is a thick mist in my eyes, which, if you can, disperse with the bright beams of reason.' Langius, with a wrinkled forehead, 'So youngster', he said, 'have you so soon gone astray again? I will have none of that. For as a skilful huntsman suffers not their hound to range, but to follow one and the same deer, so would I have you tread only in those footsteps which I have traced out to you. I would beat into your brain the ends of afflictions to the intent that if you are good, you may think yourself to be exercised; if fallen, to be lifted up; if utterly naught, to be punished. And now you draw me to the causes. Wandering mind! What do you mean by this curious carefulness? Will you need feel those celestial fires? They will melt you like wax. Will you climb up into the tower of Providence? You will soon fall down headlong. As butterflies, and other little flies do by night flutter so long about the candle, till it burns them, so does man's mind dally about that secret celestial flame.

Show me the causes, you say, why the vengeance of God skips over some and whips others? Do you seek the causes? I say most safely that I know them not. For the heavenly court never comprehended me, nor I the decrees of it. Of this only am I assured, that God's will is a cause above all causes, beyond which who so seeks another is ignorant of the efficacy and power of the divine nature. For it is necessary that every cause is in a sort before and greater than its effect, but nothing is before nor greater than God and his will, therefore there is no cause thereof. God has pardoned; God has punished; what will you have more? "The will of God is the chief justice", as Salvianus said well and godly.[141] Yet you say, we require a reason of this inequality. Of whom? Of God? To whom that is lawful whatsoever he likes; and he likes nothing but that which is lawful. If the servant calls his master or the subject his sovereign to account, the tone may take it in contempt, and the other as treason. And are you more bold with God? Begone, such perverse curiosity. "This reason cannot stand otherwise than if it be rendered to no man".[142] And yet when you have done all that you are able, you will not clear yourself out of the dark mists of ignorance, nor be partaker of those mere mystical counsels and decrees. It is excellently spoken by Sophocles, "you will never attain to the knowledge of heavenly things if God conceals them; nor of them all, though you bestow your labour ever therein".[143]

Chapter 13

Yet to certify the curious, three old objections are answered. And first touching evil men not punished. We prove they are reprived, and pardoned. And that either in respect of men themselves, or in regard of God's nature, which is slow to punish.

'This plain and broad way, Lipsius, is only safe here; all others are deceivable and slippery. In divine and heavenly matters, it is the sharpest sight to see nought, and the only knowledge to know nothing. Yet because this cloud has of old time and now does compass men's wits, I will wind you out of it shortly, if I can. And I will wash away that which sticks in you, with this river here at hand. O you celestial and eternal spirit (with which he cast his eyes on high) pardon and forgive me if in these profound mysteries I utter anything impure or ungodly, yet with a godly intent. And first I may generally defend the justice of God with his own blow. If God beholds the affairs of men, he has care of them; if he has care, he governs them; if he governs, he does it with judgement; if with judgement, how can it be without justice? Which if it be wanting there is no regiment nor government at all, but disorder, confusion, and trouble. What have you to oppose against this weapon? What shield or armour? Say the truth, only man's ignorance. I understand not, you say, why these should be punished, and those not. Well said. Will you therefore join impudence to your ignorance? And because you comprehend not the power of the divine and pure law, will you carp at it? What more unjust reason would be alleged against justice? If some stranger should utter his conjectures of the laws and ordinances of your country, you would bid him hold his tongue and be gone, because he has not the knowledge of them. And do you, an inhabitant of this earth rashly condemn the unknown laws of heaven? You creature, your creator? Yet go to, take your pleasure, I will close nearer with you, searching distinctly the thick mists of these your objections by the clear sun of reason, as you require. You object three things, that God lets offenders escape; that he punishes innocents; that he puts over and transfers his punishments from one to another. I will begin with the first.

You say that the vengeance of God does not do well to overpass the wicked. But does it overpass them? No, I think rather it forbears them only for a time. If I have great debts owing me, and if it pleases me to exact my due of one debtor presently and to bear with another for a longer time, who can blame me? For it is at my own good will and pleasure. Even so does that great God; of whom whereas all naughty men have deserved punishment, he exacts it of some presently, and bears with others to be paid afterwards with interest. What unrighteousness is here, except it be so that you take thought for God, and fear lest he be indemnified by this his bountiful forbearance. But alas silly man! You are more afraid than hurt. Never shall any man deceive this great creditor. Wherever we fly, we are all in his sight, in bonds and fetters to him. But you say, I would have such a tyrant to be presently punished, that by his death at this time, satisfaction may be made to so many whom he has oppressed. So shall the justice of God be made more manifest to us. No, by this you betray your blockishness. For who are you that does not only appoint God how but also prescribe him when to punish? Do you think that he is your judge, or only a sergeant or under-officer? Go, lead him hence, whip him, muffle his face, hang him upon a cursed tree, for so it seems good in my eyes. What impudency! To God it seems otherwise, whom you must understand to see much better in this case than yourself, and to have another end in punishing. You are provoked with anger and carried away with desire of revenge. He, being far from both these, has respect to the example and correction of others. He also knows best to whom the same may do good and when. The moments often are of great weight, and the most wholesome medicine if often turned to the destruction of the diseased, not being applied in due season. God cut off Caligula in the prime of his tyranny. He suffered Nero to run on farther; and Tiberius farthest of all. And do not doubt that it was for the good of those that then murmured at it. Our evil and disordered manners have need of a continual scourge, but we would have it taken from us at the first, and cast into the fire. This is one cause of forebearance, which respects us.

Another there is in respect of God, to whom it seems peculiar. To proceed slowly in revenge of himself, and to quit that slackness with the grievousness of the punishment. Well spoke Sinesius, "the divine nature proceeds leisurely and orderly".[144] And the old sages went not much awry, who in this respect feigned God to have woollen feet so that although you be a hasty man and given to revenge, you ought not to be grieved at this forbearance which is such a delay of the punishment, as it is withal an increasing of the same. Tell me, in beholding a tragedy, will it stomach you to see Atreus or Thyestes in the first or second act walking in state and majesty upon the scene? To see them reign, threat, and command? I think not, knowing their prosperity to be of small continuance; and when you will see them shamefully come to confusion in the last act. Now then in this tragedy of the world, why are you not so favourable towards God as to a poor poet? This wicked man prospers. That tyrant lives. Let be awhile. Remember it is but the first act, and consider aforehand in your mind that sobs and sorrows will ensue upon their solace. This scene will anon swim in blood, then these purple and golden garments shall be rolled therein. For that poet of ours is singularly cunning in his art and will not lightly transgress the laws of his tragedy. In music, do we not allow sometimes disagreeing sounds, knowing that they will all close in consent? But the parties injured do not always see the punishment. What marvel is that? The tragedy commonly is tedious, and they are not able to sit so long in the theatre; yet others do see it, and are worthily stricken with fear when they perceive that some are reprieved before this severe throne of justice, but not pardoned. And that the day of execution is prolonged, not wholly taken away. Wherefore, Lipsius, hold this for certain, that ungodly men are forborne awhile, but never forgiven; and that no man has a sin in his heart, but the same man carries Nemesis on his back. For that fury follows them always, and as I may say with Euripides, "going silently and with a soft foot, she will in due time violently pluck the wicked from off the earth".[145]

Chapter 14

Then it is shown that there are sundry kinds of punishments; and some of them hidden or inward, always accompanying the wicked facts themselves, which ungodly men shall never escape. And they are more grievous than any outward.

'Yet to make you conceive these things better, and that I may lead you at length into the chief bulwark of this argument, you must understand that there are three sundry sorts of God's punishments; internal, after this life, external. The first I call those that vex the mind or soul yet coupled to the body; as sorrow, repentance, fear, and a thousand gnawings of conscience. The second sort are such as touch the same soul being free and loosed from the body; as be those punishments which most of the old heathen writers did (not without reason) conjecture were reserved for ungodly men after this life. The third which touch the body, or are about the same; as poverty, banishment, griefs, diseases, death. And it comes to pass often that all these, by the just judgement of God, do fall upon the wicked. But certainly the two former kinds do always follow them. And to speak of internal punishments, what man was there at any time so given over to work wickedness that he felt in his mind sharp scourges, and (as it were) heavy strokes either in committing mischievous deeds, or else after the facts committed? For Plato said truly, "that punishment is the companion of injustice".[146] Or as Hesiod more plainly and forcibly expresses the matter, "it is coeternal and coequal with it".[147] The punishment of wickedness is kin to every wicked act, and bred in it; neither is anything free and out of care in this life but innocence. As malefactors among the Romans that were condemned to be crucified did bear their cross, which soon after should bear them, so has God laid this cross of conscience upon all ungodly men, whereby they may suffer pains before they come to execution. Do you think there is no other punishment but that which is objected to our eyes? Or that which is inflicted upon the body? It is far otherwise. All such are external, and do lightly for a short time only touch us. But those that are inward do torment us. As we judge those to be more sick who pine away with a consumption, than those that have an inflammation or fever, and yet these last have the greatest appearance; even so are those wicked men in a worse case, who are led to everlasting death with a lingering pace. Caligula ruling with great tyranny would be so stricken on a sudden as though he should die. So fares it with those wickedlings when that butcher (their own mind) pricks and beats continually with soft strokes.

Let not the gorgeous outward appearance beguile you, nor the mighty pomp in which they are environed, or their abundance of wealth. For they are not the happier nor in any better case thereby, no more than a sick man whose fever or gout lies upon a stately feather bed. When you see a poor beggarly fellow playing a king's part on a stage, adorned with golden robes, you envy him not, knowing that under the same gorgeous attire are scabs, filth, and uncleanness; have you the very same opinion of all these great proud tyrants, "whose minds if they might be opened (says Tacitus) we should behold tears and strokes; from that even as the body with stripes, so is the mind torn in pieces with cruelty, lust, and evil thoughts".[148] I know they laugh sometimes, but it is only from the teeth outward. They rejoice, but with no true joy. No more certainly than they who, being in a dungeon condemned to die, do seek to beguile themselves with playing at dice or tables, and yet cannot. For the deep imprinted terror of punishment at hand remains, and the image of grisly death never departs from before their eyes. I pray you draw back this curtain of external things, and behold that Sicilian tyrant,[149]

> Over whose wicked head a naked sword
> Does always hang.[150]

Listen to that Roman emperor lamentably crying out "all the gods and goddesses send me a worse destruction than that I feel a daily dying in me".[151] Hear another of them sighing from the heart, and saying, "What? Am I the only man that has neither friend nor foe?"[152] These are the true torments of the mind, Lipsius. These are gripping griefs indeed, always to be vexed, sorrowful, terrified. Beware you do not compare any tortures, racks, or iron instruments to these.'

Chapter 15

That pains after this life are prepared for evildoers. And most commonly also external punishments. Confirmed by some notable examples.[153]

'Join moreover to this those everlasting pains after this life, which

it suffices me only to point at out of the midst of divinity, without
further unfolding of them. Add also external punishments, which if
they be wanting, yet inasmuch as the former never are omitted, who
can rightly blame the justice of God? But I say that those first are
not lacking. And never, or surely very seldom does it happen that
notorious evil persons and such as oppress others, do suffer open and
public pains. Some of them sooner, some later; some in themselves,
and some in their posterity. You mark and murmur that the Sicilian
tyrant Dionysius does for many years together commit adulteries,
rapes, murders, without control. Have patience a little while, you will
see him shortly infamous, a banished man, beggarly, and (a matter
scarcely credible) thrust down from the sceptre to the cane.[154] The
same king of a great island shall set up a school at Corinth, himself
being indeed a very scoff to fortune. On the other side, does it grieve
you that Pompey should be overthrown in Pharsalia, and his army
almost consisting of senators? That the tyrant should take his pleasure
and pastime while in the blood of citizens? I blame you not much,
considering that Cato himself here lost the helm of sound judgement,
and from his heart uttered this doubtful voice, "divine matters are full
of obscurity".[155] Notwithstanding you Lipsius, you Cato, cast your
eyes a little aside, you shall see one thing that will bring you into good
liking with God again. Behold that Caesar, stately, a conqueror, in his
own and some other folks' opinion, a very god; slain in, and of the
senate. And that not with one simple death, but wounded with three
and twenty several thrusts, and rolling in his own blood like a beast.
And (what more could you wish?) this was done even in the court of
Pompey, the image of Pompey standing there on high, celebrating a
great sacrifice to the ghost of that great one. Even so, Brutus losing
his life in the Philippian fields for his country, and with his country,
moves me to compassion. But I am recomforted when I see not only
after those conquering armies (as it were) before his tomb falling
together by the ears between themselves, and master Mark Antony
one of the chieftains overcome both by sea and land, among three
silly women hardly finding death with that womanish hand. Where
are you now that of late was lord of all the east? Leader of the
Roman armies? Persecutor of Pompey and the commonwealth? Lo,
you hang in a rope by your bloody hands! Lo, you creep into your
grave half alive! Lo, dying you cannot be withdrawn from her who

was your death! Mark whether Brutus uttered in vain those last words at his death, "O Jupiter, let not the author of this evil beguile you".[156] No more did he deceive or escape him. No more did that other captain, who not obscurely suffered in himself the punishment of his youthful misdeeds. But yet more apparently in all his progeny. Let him by happy and mighty Caesar, and truly Augustus. But with all let him have a daughter Julia, and a niece; also some of his nephews let him lose by false accusations. Others let him banish out of his favour. And with loathsomeness of these let him wish to die with four days hunger, and not be able. Finally, let him live with his Livia, unhonestly married, unhonestly kept. And upon whom he doted with unlawful love, let him die a shameful death by her means. In conclusion, said Pliny, "he being made a god and gaining heaven (but I know not whether he deserved it) let him die, and let the son of his enemy be his heir".[157] These and such like things, Lipsius, are to be thought upon whensoever we begin to break forth into any complaints of unrighteousness in God. And we must always cast our minds to the consideration of two things, the slowness and the diversity of punishments. Is not such a man punished? Hold contented a little, he shall feel it before long; if not in his body, yet assuredly in his mind. If not while he lives, yet doubtless when he is dead.

> Though vengeance comes behind and her foot sore,
> She overtakes the offender that goes before.[158]

For that same heavenly eye watches still, and when you think it sleeps soundly, it does but wink a little. Only see that you bear yourself uprightly towards him; and do not vainly accuse your judge by whom you yourself must soon be judged.'

Chapter 16

An answer to the other objection touching guiltless men. It is proved that all have deserved punishment, for that all are offenders. And who they be that do offend more or less, can hardly or by no means be discerned by men. It is God only that sees thoroughly into faults, and therefore does punish most justly.

But you say that guiltless and innocent people are punished. For this is your second complaint, or rather I may term it a slanderous accusation. Unadvised young man! So speak you? In what country may we find such countrymen as are without fault? It was great boldness, even rashness to affirm that of any one man. And do you make no scruple to quit whole peoples and nations of offence? You do most foolishly. I know we have all sinned and daily do; we are born in uncleanness and in it we live. Insomuch that the storehouse of heaven (as I may say with the Satirist) would be without thunderbolts if they were hurled continually upon all that do offend.[159] For though fishes be engendered and nourished in the salt sea and themselves taste not of any saltiness, yet may we not think it to be so with us men, that we being born in this contagion of the world should ourselves be without corruption. Then if all be offenders, where are these harmless innocent people? For punishment is always most justly the companion of offence.

But you will say, I dislike the inequality, in that some folk having trespassed but a little are grievously corrected, and others notoriously naughty are suffered to flourish and have dominion. I see what the matter is. You would like to take the balance of justice out of God's hand and will poise it after your own fantasy and pleasure. To what else tends this your valuation of greater or smaller offences, which you assume to you before God? But here, Lipsius, I would have you consider two things; first that men cannot nor ought to take upon them the judging of other's faults. For how can it be that you, silly man, should weigh faults uprightly, which does not mark them thoroughly? Can you give sentence justly of that which you are not able to examine diligently? You will easily grant that it is the mind or soul which sins, by means of the body and the instruments of the senses, but yet so that the whole weight and burden of sin rests upon it. This is so true that if you grant a man has committed ought against his will, then he has not therein sinned. If it is so, how are you able to behold the offence, when you see not so much as the harbour and the seat thereof? And surely you are so far from seeing another man's mind that you perceive not your own. Therefore this is great folly or temerity in arrogating to yourself the censuring and judgement of that thing which is not seen, nor to be seen; neither known nor able to be comprehended by any man's knowledge.

Secondly, admit there is such inequality as you speak of; yet there is no harm nor wrong done here. No harm, in that it is for their good which are presently punished even for their least faults. Therein God loves us. And we ought greatly to misdoubt long forbearance, whichever brings with it more grievous pains. Again, neither is there any wrong done thereby, because (as I said) we have all of us deserved punishment, and there is not in the best any such purity, but that some spots do stain them which must be washed away with this salt water of adversities. Wherefore, young man, let pass this most intricate disputation of the estimating of faults and offences, you being an earthly and very simple judge. Refer it to God, who discerns more uprightly and soundly that matter from his high throne of justice. He alone it is that esteems indifferently of defects; he who without any fraud or daubing of dissimulation beholds virtue and vice in their proper hue. Who can deceive him who searches all outward and inward things alike, who sees both body and mind? The tongue and the very veins of the heart? Finally all things whether open or secret? Who sees not only the deeds done, but even the causes and proceedings of them as clear as the noon light. Thales, being once demanded whether anyone could beguile God that did commit wickedness? "No, nor if he do, he but imagine it only."[160] So he said truly. But now it is otherwise with us being here in darkness, who not only do not see secret sins, but also such as are done under the coat and skirts, as they say, no nor scarce those that be manifest and committed in the daylight. For we do not discern the fault itself and the whole force thereof, but only some external signs of the same, when it is done and has turned its back to be gone again. We do often think them the best men whom God knows to be the worst; and we reject those whom he does elect. Wherefore, if you have wisdom, shut your eyes and stop your mouth from having anything to do touching the worthiness or unworthiness of men. Such hidden causes are hardly known for certain.'

Chapter 17

An answer to the third objection touching punishments translated or put off from one person to another. It is shown by examples that the same is usually done among men. What is the cause wherefore God uses such translating of punishments from one to another. Also certain other matters full of subtle curiosity.

'But now the third cloud brought in to overshadow God's justice must be blown away. For some say that God does not deal uprightly in shifting over punishments from one to another. Neither is it well that the posterity should suffer pains for the faults of their predecessors. What? Is that such a rare or strange matter? No, rather I marvel why these men should marvel at that, seeing they do even the same here in this world. Tell me in good truth, do not the rewards that princes bestow upon the ancestors for their virtues remain and extend also to their posterity? Surely they do. And I think the like of revenge and punishment for their evil deservings. Behold in cases of treason against the state or person of a prince, some are apparently in the fault, and others do communicate with them in the punishment. Which thing is so far intended by man's security, as it is provided by laws that the innocent children should be punished with perpetual poverty; "so as death may seem a solace to them and life a scourge".[161] Your minds are altogether malicious. You will permit that to some king or petty potentate which you will not to God, who notwithstanding if you consider it well, has far greater reason for this severity. For we have transgressed and rebelled against this mighty king every one of us; and by many descents is that first blemish or stain derived to the unhappy children; such a chaining and linking together of offences there is before God. Neither was it my father or yours that first began to sin, but the father of all fathers. What marvel is it then if he punishes in the posterity those faults which are not properly diverse, but by certain communication of seed made joint, and never being discontinued.

But to let pass these high mysteries, and to deal with you by a more familiar kind of reasoning; know this, that God joins together those things which we through frailty or ignorance do separate and put asunder, and that he beholds families, towns, kingdoms, not as things confused or distinguished, but as one body and entire nature. The family of the Scipios or Caesars is but one whole thing to him. The city of Rome or Athens, during all the time of their continuance, one. So likewise the Roman empire. And there is good reason it should be so. For there is a certain bond of laws and communion of rights that knits together these great bodies, which causes a participation of rewards and punishments to be between those that have lived in diverse ages. Therefore, were the Scipios good men in times past? Their posterity shall speed the better for it before the heavenly judge. Were they evil? Let their posterity fare the worse. Have the Flemings not many years past been lascivious, covetous, godless? Let us smart for it. Because in all external punishments God does not only behold the time present, but also has respect to time past. And so by pondering of both these together, he poises evenly the balance of his justice. I said in all "external punishments", and I would have you mark it well. For the faults of one man are not laid upon another, neither is there any confusion of offences (God forbid that). But these are only pains and chastisements about us, not in us, and properly do concern the body or goods, but not our mind which is internal. And what injury at all is there in this? We will be heirs to our ancestors of commodities and rewards, if they deserve any. Why should we refuse their punishments and pains? "O Romans, you shall suffer punishments for the offences of your predecessors, unworthily."[162] So said the Roman poet, and he spoke true, but only in that he added "unworthily". For it is most deservedly, because their forefathers had deserved it. But the poet saw the effect only, without lifting up his consideration to the cause. Notwithstanding as one and the self same man may lawfully abide punishment in his old age for some offence committed in his youth, even so in empires and kingdoms does God punish old sins because that in respect of outward communication and society they are but one selfsame thing before God. These distances often do not separate us in his sight, who has all eternity enclosed in his infinite capacity. Did those martial wolves in old times overthrow so many towns, and break in pieces so many sceptres scot-free? Have they sucked so much blood by slaughter, and themselves never lost their blood? Then I will surely confess that God is no revenger "who both hears and sees whatsoever we do".[163] But the case stands otherwise. For it cannot be but they must at length even in their posterity receive punishment, though slow, yet never too late.

Neither is there with God this conjunction and uniting of times only, but of parts also. This is my meaning: that like as in man when the hands, the secret parts, and belly do transgress, the whole body buys the bargain dearly, so in a common multitude the sin of a few is often required at the hands of all. Especially if the offenders be the worthiest members as kings, princes, and magistrates. Well said Hesiod, and out of the bowels of wisdom:

> For one man's fault the city suffers pain,
> When one commits sacrilege or wrong;
> From heaven God makes tempests down to rain,
> Or pestilence, or famishment among.[164]

So the whole Greek navy perished for one man's offence, even the furious outrage of Ajax Oileus. Likewise in Jewry seventy thousand men were justly consumed with one plague, for the unlawful lust of the king.[165] Sometimes it falls out contrarily, that whereas all have sinned, God chooses out one or a few to be, as it were, a sacrifice for the common crime. In which although he declines a little from the straight level of equality, yet of this inequality a new kind of justice arises. And the same which in a few seems to be rigour, is a certain merciful righteousness towards many. Does not the schoolmaster's cane correct one among a multitude of loitering scholars? Does not a general in the wars punish his mutinous army by drawing the tenth man?[166] And both these do it upon good advice, for that this punishment inflicted upon a few does terrify and amend all. I see physicians many times open a vein in the foot or arm when the whole body is distempered. What know I whether it be so in this case? For these matters be mysteries, Lipsius. They be very deep mysteries. If we are wise let us not come too near this sacred fire whose sparks and small flakes we men perchance may see, but not the thing itself. Even as they who fix their eyes too seriously upon the sun do lose them, so we extinguish all the light of our mind by beholding earnestly this light. My opinion, therefore, is that we ought to abstain from this curious question so full of danger, and be resolved of this, that mortal men cannot rightfully judge of offences, nor ought not to attempt it. God has another manner of balance, and another tribunal seat of justice. And howsoever those secret judgements of his be executed, we must not accuse but suffer and reverence them. This one sentence I would have you to be thoroughly persuaded of, with which I shall shut up this matter and stop the mouths of all curious busybodies: "the most part of God's judgements are secret, but none of them unrighteous".'[167]

Chapter 18

A passage to the last place, which is of examples. It is shown to be a matter profitable often to mix some things of sweet taste with sharper medicines.

'This much, Lipsius, I had to say in defence of God's justice against unjust accusers, which I confess was not altogether pertinent to my purpose, and yet not much besides it; because doubtless we shall the more willingly and indifferently bear these great public miseries when we are fully persuaded they be justly inflicted upon us.' And here pausing our communication awhile, Langius suddenly broke out into these words: 'It is well, I have taken breath a little. And being now passed beyond all the dangerous rocks of difficult questions, it seems I may with full sails strike into the haven. I behold here at hand my fourth and last troop, which I intend willingly to bring into the field. And as mariners being in a tempest, when they see the two twins appear together,[168] do receive great hope and comfort, so fares it with me, to whom after many sturdy storms, this double legion has shown itself. Let me lawfully term it so, after the ancient manner, because it is forked or twofold. And by it I must manfully prove two several things, that these evils which now we suffer are neither grievous, nor new and unaccustomed. In certain of which few matters that are left unhandled, I pray you, Lipsius, show yourself willing and attentive to me.' 'Never more willing, Langius, than now. For it pleases me very well that we have passed through the pikes; and I long earnestly for some pleasant and familiar medicines, after these sharp and bitter pills. And so it appears by the title that the disputation ensuing will be.' 'You say true', said

Langius. 'And even as the surgeons after they have seared and cut as much as they like, do not forthwith dismiss their patient, but apply some gentle medicines and comfortable salves to assuage the pain, so I having sufficiently seared and purged you with the razors and fire of wisdom, will now cherish you again with some sweeter communication, and will touch you with a milder hand, as the saying is. I will descend from that craggy hill of philosophy, leading you awhile into the pleasant fields of philology. And that, not so much for your recreation as for your health. It is said that Demochares, a physician having for his patient Considia, a noble woman who refused all kinds of sharp medicines, ministered to her the milk of goats, which he caused to feed altogether upon mastic.[169] So it is my purpose to impart now to you some historical and delectable matters, but yet sauced with a secret liquor of wisdom. What matter is it which way we attempt the curing of a sick body, so long as we restore him to perfect health?'

Chapter 19

That public evils are not as grievous as they seem to be; which first is briefly proved by reason. For most commonly we fear the circumstances and adjuncts of things, more than the things themselves.

'Now march forwards my own good legion. And first of all that troop which are assigned to the forward, proving that these evils are not grievous, which we shall convince by a twofold argument, of reason and comparison. Of Reason, because if you have due respect to it, truly all these things which do befall us and hang over our heads, are neither grievous nor great, but do only seem so to be. It is Opinion which does augment and amplify them, and lifts them up as it were upon a stage to be seen. But if you are wise, scatter abroad that thick mist, and behold the things in the clear light. For example's sake, you in this time of public calamities fear poverty, banishment, and death. If you look upon these things with indifferent and sound eyes, alas, what trifles are they? If you poise them according to their weight, how light are they? This war, or else the tyranny of governors through excessive tributes will impoverish you. What then? You will be a poor man. Did not nature so make you, and so shall take you hence? But if the odious and infamous name of tyranny offends you, change your habitation, so shall you free yourself. Fortune, if you mark it, has helped you, and provided you a place of more security. No man shall pillage you any more. Thus the thing which you did account as damage shall be a remedy to you. "But I shall be a banished man." No, rather a stranger, if you will. If you alter your affection, you change your country. A wise man, in whatever place he is, is as a pilgrim. And a fool, wherever he goes, is an exile.

But you will say, death is daily imminent to me by means of a tyrant. As though it were not so every day by nature. "Yes but it is a shameful matter to die by execution or strangling." O fool, neither that nor any other kind of death is infamous, except if your life be such. Recount to me the best and worthiest persons that have been since the beginning of the world; they ended their lives by violence.[170] This examination, Lipsius, of which I do give you a taste only, must be used in all those things which do seem terrible, and we must behold them naked without any vestment or mask of opinions. But we poor wretches do turn ourselves to these vain and external matters, not fearing the things themselves but the circumstances and adjuncts of them. Behold, if you sail on the sea, and it begins to swell mightily, your courage quails, and you tremble with fear, as though if your ship were cast away you should swallow up the whole sea, whereas one quart or two of it will suffice to drown you.[171] If an earthquake is suddenly raised, what crying out and quaking is there? You imagine that the whole town, or at least a house, will fall upon you, and do not consider that the dropping down of one little stone is enough to knock out your brains. Even so is it in these great common calamities, in which the noise and vain imagination of things does terrify us. "See this troop of soldiers! See these shining swords!" Why? What can these soldiers or these swords do? "They will kill me." What is killing? A bare and mere death only. And that the name may not terrify you, it is but a departure of the soul from the body. All that bands of soldiers, all that threatening swords shall do, but which one fever, one small seed of a grape, or one little worm may bring to pass.

"But the other is more painful." No, it is far more easy, for a fever

which you seem rather to choose, keeps a man in pains commonly a
whole year together, but here the matter is ended with one blow in
a moment. Therefore it was well spoken of Socrates, who used to
call all these things nothing other but "goblins" or painted masks,[172]
which if you put on, children run from you frightened, but so soon
as you put off the same and show your own face, they will come
about you and embrace you in their arms. Even so stands the case
in these matters that seem so terrible, which if you behold without
veil or mask, you will confess that all your fear was but childish.
As hailstones though they beat upon houses with a great noise, yet
themselves do leap away and are dissolved, so these things if they
happen to light upon a constant settled mind, do not cast down it,
but vanish and come to naught themselves.'

Chapter 20

*Now we come to comparison. And first of all the misery of the
Low Countries and of this our age is exaggerated. That opinion
is generally confuted. And it is declared how that the natural
disposition of men is prone to augment their own griefs.*

This earnest and grave communication of Langius was nothing
answerable to my hope or expectation. Wherefore interrupting him,
'Where now?', I said, 'Was this your promise to me? I expected the
sweet wine and honeycombs of histories, but you serve me with
such sour sauce as there is none more sharp among all the store
of philosophy. What? Do you think that you have to do with some
Thales? No, no. Now you have Lipsius in hand, who as he is a man,
and of the common sort of men, so he desires remedies somewhat
more spiced with humanity than these are.' Then, Langius said with
a mild voice and countenance, 'I confess indeed I am worthy of
blame. For in following the bright beams of reason, I see myself to
have strayed out of the highway and declined unawares into the path
of wisdom again. But now I will amend the matter, and return to
hold on my course in a more familiar known trade-path. Does the
sharpness of the wine that I broached dislike you? I will sweeten it
with the honey of examples. Now therefore I come to comparisons,

and will prove evidently that there is nothing grievous or great in all these evils which are now about everywhere, if we compare them with those of old time. For in times past the same have been far more heinous and lamentable than now.' At this I once again more eagerly than before replied, 'What? Say you so indeed? "And think you to bring me into that belief?"'[173] No, Langius, not so long as there is any sense in my head. For what age past, if you examine the matter rightly, has at any time been so miserable as this ours, or even shall be? What country, what region has suffered, "so many things grievous to be spoken of and rigorous to be endured",[174] as we Flemings do at this day? We are shaken to and fro with wars not only foreign but civil; and not such only, but even within our own bowels. For there are not only parties among us, but new parties of these same parties. Alas, my dear country, what safety can save you? Add to this pestilence, and famine, tributes, rapes, slaughters; also the "uttermost extremity"[175] of tyranny. And oppressions not of bodies only, but also of minds. And what is there in other parts of Europe? War, or fear of war. And if any peace be, it is joined with shameful servitude under petty lords, and no better at all than any kind of war. Wherever we cast our eyes or thoughts, all things hang in suspense and suspicion. And, as it were in an old ruinous house, there be many tokens of falling down. In sum, Langius, like as all rivers run into the sea, so it seems that all misfortunes are fallen upon this present age. I speak only of those evils which are in action, and now presently tossing us. What need I make mention of such as hang over our heads? To which I may truly apply that saying of Euripides:

> I see so great a sea of evils nigh at hand,
> So that it seems a matter hard safely to swim to land.'[176]

Langius, turning himself towards me angrily, and as it were with intent to rebuke me, 'What? Do you yet again cast yourself down by these complaints? I thought you had stood fast like a man, and I see you fall; that your wounds had been quite closed up, but I perceive you do open them again. How is it you must be endowed with peace of mind if you will be in perfect health.

You say this age is the unhappiest that ever was. This has been an old accusation long ago used. I know your grandfather said so, and likewise your father. I know also that your children and children's children will sing the same note. It is a thing naturally given to men to cast their eyes narrowly upon all things that are grievous, but to wink at such as be pleasant. As flies and such like vile creatures do never rest long upon smooth and fine polished places, but do stick fast to rough and filthy corners, so the murmuring mind does lightly pass over the consideration of all good fortune but never forgets the adverse or evil. It handles and pries into that, and often augments it with great wit. Like as lovers do always behold something in their mistress by which they think her to excel all others, even so do men that mourn in their miseries. Moreover, we imagine things that are false, and bewail not only things present, but also such as are to come. And what gain we by this forereaching wit of ours? Surely nothing else but that as some spying a far off dust raised by an army do thereupon forsake their tents for fear, so the vain shadow of future danger casts us down into the pit of desperation.'

Chapter 21

The same is more properly and precisely confuted by comparison with the evils of old time. First of the wars and marvelous desolations of the Jews.

'But you, Lipsius, let pass these vulgar matters, and follow me now to that comparison which you so much desire. Thereby it shall most plainly appear to you that the miserable desolations of old time were not only in all respects equal to these of our age, but did far surpass them; and that we who live in these days have cause to rejoice rather than to grudge. You say we are tossed with wars. What then? Were not they of old time likewise? Yes, Lipsius, they had their beginning with the world, and shall never be at an end so long as the world lasts. But perhaps theirs were not so great, nor so grievous as ours are. No, but it is so far otherwise that all ours are mere jestings and toys (I speak in good earnest) if they be compared with the ancient ages. I shall hardly find an entrance in, or a way out, if once I throw myself into this deep sea of examples. Notwithstanding, shall we wander a little through all parts of the world? Let us go. We will begin with Judea, that is, with the holy nation and people. I let pass those things which they suffered in Egypt and immediately after their departure from there, for they are recorded and may easily be seen in Holy Scripture. I will come to the last of all, even such as are annexed to their final destruction, which it is expedient that I propound particularly as it were in the manner of a table. They suffered therefore in civil and foreign wars within the space of seven years, these things ensuing:

First there were slain at Jerusalem by the commandment of Florus – 630

At Caesarea by the inhabitants there, for hatred of the nation and their religion, at once – 20,000

At Scithopolis, a town of Syria – 13,000

At Ascalon in Palestina, of the inhabitants there – 2,500

Also at Ptolomais – 2,000

At Alexandria in Egypt, under Tiberius Alexander then president – 50,000

At Damascus – 10,000

And all this happened as it were by sedition and tumults. Afterwards, by lawful and open war with the Romans:

When Joppa was taken by Cesius Florus, there were slain of them – 8,400

Also in Mount Cabulon – 2,000

In fight at Ascalon – 10,000

Again by deceit – 8,000

At the taking of Aphaca – 15,000

In Mount Gazarin were slain – 11,600

At Jotapa, where Josephus himself was, about – 30,000

Again at the taking of Joppa, were drowned – 4,200

In Tarichaeis slain – 6,500

At Gamala killed, and that wilfully cast themselves headlong down from steep places – 9,000, and not one man born in that town escaped, save two women that were sisters.

Giscala being abandoned, there were slain in the fight – 2,000

And of women and children taken captives – 3,000

Of the Gaderens were put to the sword – 13,000

Taken captives – 2,200. Besides an infinite number that leapt into the river.

In the streets of Idumaea were killed – 10,000
At Gerasium – 1,000
At Macheruns – 1,700[177]
In the wood Iarde – 3,000
In Massada a little castle were slain wilfully by themselves – 960
In Cirene slain by Catulus the president – 3,000
But in the city of Jerusalem during all the time of the siege, there died
     and were killed – 1,000,000[178]
Taken captives – 97,000
This whole sum, besides an innumerable company not spoken of,
     amounts to – 1,339,690[179]

What do you say, Lipsius? Do you cast down your eyes at this? No, rather lift them up, and see whether you dare again compare the wars that have been throughout all Christendom these many years, with the miserable desolations of this one Jewish nation.'

Chapter 22

Of the destructions of the Greeks and Romans by war. The great numbers of them that have been slain by certain captains. Also the wasting of the new world. And the extreme miseries of captivity.

'I rest not here, but hold my way forwards into Greece. And if I should recount in order all the wars that those people have had among themselves at home, or abroad with others, it would be tedious to tell, and without any profit. Thus much only I say, that this region has continually been so wasted and hacked with the sword of calamity, as Plutarch records (which I never read without anger and admiration) that the whole nation in his time was not able to make three thousand soldiers.[180] And yet, he said, in times past even in the Persian War, one little town by Athens called Megara sufficed to raise that number. Alas how are you decayed? O you garden of the whole earth? The glory and beauty of nations. There is scarce now a town of any name in this distressed country of Belgica that cannot match that number of warlike people. Now shall we take a view of the Romans and of Italy? Augustine and Orosius have already eased me of this business in rehearsing. See their writings, and in them huge seas of evils.[181] One Carthaginian war, even the second within the country of Italy, Spain, and Sicily, and within the space of 17 years consumed fourteen hundred thousand men and above (for I have searched the number very narrowly). The civil war between Caesar and Pompey, 300,000. And the weapons of Brutus, Cassius, and Sextus Pompeius, more than that. What speak I of wars managed under the conduct of diverse persons? Behold. Only Caesar (O the plague and pestilence of mankind!) confesses and that with boasting "that he slew in battles eleven hundred ninety and two thousand men".[182] And yet the butchery of his civil wars runs not in this reckoning. These slaughters were committed upon foreigners in those few years in which he ruled over Spain and France. And yet notwithstanding in this respect he who was surnamed "the Great"[183] surpassed him, who caused it to be written in the temple of Minerva that he had overcome, put to flight, slain, and upon yielding received to mercy, twenty hundred four score and four thousand men. And to make up the account, added to these, if you will, Q. Fabius who slew 110,000 Frenchmen, C. Marius 200,000 Cimbrians, and in a later age Aetius, who in a famous battle killed a hundred three score and two thousand Hungarians.

Neither do you imagine that men only were destroyed in these great wars, but likewise good towns were ruined by them. Cato surnamed Censorius boasted that he took more towns in Spain than he had been days in that country.[184] Sempronius Gracchus, if we give credit to Polybius, utterly overthrew thirty in the same region. I think that no age since the world began is able to match these, but only ours, yet in another world. A few Spaniards sailing within these fourscore years into that marvellous wide new world,[185] O good God, what exceeding great slaughters have they wrought? What wonderful desolations? I speak not of the causes and equity of the war, but only of the events. I behold that huge scope of ground (a great matter to have seen, I say not to have subdued it) how it was walked through by twenty or thirty soldiers. And these naked herds of people cut down by them, even as corn with a scythe. Where are you the most mighty island of Cuba? You Haiti? You Bahamas? – which before being replenished with five or six hundred thousand men, in some of you scant fifteen are left alive to preserve your

seed. Show yourself awhile, Peru and Mexico. O marvellous and
miserable spectacle! That mighty large country, and in truth another
world, appears desolate and wasted, no otherwise than if it had been
consumed with fire from heaven. My mind and tongue both do fail
me, Lipsius, in recounting these matters; and I see all our troubles
in comparison with those to be nothing else but small fragments of
straw, or, as the comic poet says, little mites.[186]

And yet have I not spoken at all of the condition of captive
slaves, than the which nothing was more miserable in the ancient
wars. Free born men, noble men, children, women, all whatsoever
they were did the conqueror carry away. And who knows whether
they were led into perpetual servitude or not? And truly the same
such a miserable kind of slavery, as I have good cause to rejoice that
not so much as the resemblance of any such has before been, nor
at this time is in Christendom. The Turks indeed do practise it, and
there is no other thing that makes that Scythian sovereignty more
odious and terrible to us.'

Chapter 23

*Most memorable examples of pestilence and famine in old times
past. Also the intolerable tributes that have been then; and the
ravenous pillaging.*

'Yet you proceed on in your whining complaint, adjoining moreover
plague and famine, tributes and rapes. Let us therefore make
comparison of all these, but in few words. Tell me, how many
thousands have died of the pestilence in all the Low Countries
within these five or six years? I think fifty or at the most one hundred
thousand. But one plague in Judea in the time of king David swept
away seventy thousand in less space than one whole day.[187] Under
the emperors Gallus and Volusianus a plague beginning in Ethiopia
went through all the Roman provinces and continued wasting and
devouring fifteen years altogether.[188] I never read of a pestilence
greater than that for continuance of time, or scope of places where
it raged. Notwithstanding for fierceness and extreme violence, that
pestilence was more notorious which reigned in Byzantium and

the places confining, under the Emperor Justinian. The extremity of which plague was so outrageous that it made every day 5,000 corpses, and some days 10,000. I would be afraid for suspicion of falsehood to write this, except I had very credible witnesses of this that lived in the same age.[189] No less wonderful was the plague of Africa which began around the subversion of Carthage. In the region of Numidia only (now called Barbary) it consumed eight hundred thousand men.[190] In the maritime coasts of Africa 200,000. And at Utica 30,000 soldiers which were left there for defence of that coast. Again in Greece under the reign of Michael Duca the plague was so hot, "that the living sufficed not to bury the dead".[191] Those are the words of Zonaras. Finally in Petrarch's time, as he records, the pestilence waxed so fervently in Italy that of every thousand persons only ten were left alive.

And now touching famine, our age has seen none in comparison of old time. Under Honorius the emperor there was such scarcity and lack of provisions at Rome that one man fed upon another, and in the place of the common assembly to see plays and games, there was heard a voice openly saying, "set a price upon man's flesh".[192] Again throughout all Italy. What time as the Goths ransacked it under Justinian, there raged so sore a famine that in the country of Picenum fifty thousand men perished with hunger. And not only the flesh but the very excrements of men served commonly for meat. Two women (I quake to speak it) killed seventeen men in the night by treachery and did eat them; at length they themselves were slain by the eighteenth, who perceived the matter.[193] I speak not of the famine in the holy city, nor of other examples commonly known.

And now if I shall say somewhat concerning tributes, it cannot be denied that they are very grievous with which we are oppressed, if we consider them in themselves alone without comparing the same with those of old times. Almost every province under the Roman empire paid yearly a fifth of their pasture land, and a tenth of their arable. Neither did Anthony and Caesar stick to exact the tributes of nine or ten years altogether in one year. After the killing of Julius Caesar, when arms were taken for defence of liberty, every citizen was commanded to defray the five and twentieth part of all his goods; and more than this, as many as were of the degree of senators paid six asses for every tilestone of their houses, which amounts to an infinite sum of money, and in our opinions neither credible nor payable.

But Octavianus Caesar, I believe, in regard of his name, exacted and received of his enfranchised servants the eighth part of all their goods. I omit that which the Triumviri and other tyrants practised, lest by the rehearsal of which I should instruct them of our time. Let one example of pillaging serve for all the rest, namely that of colonies, which device as it was most assured for the strengthening of the Empire, so there could be nothing imagined more heavy to the subjects that were conquered. Whole legions and bands of old soldiers were sent abroad into countries and towns, and the poor natural inhabitants there were in a short time fleeced of all their goods and substance, and that without any fault or offence by them, but only their wealth and fat fields were the cause. In which one kind of pillaging is contained a gulf of all calamities besides. Is it a miserable case to be spoiled of our money? What is it then to be deprived of our fields and houses? If it is grievous to be thrust out of them, what is it to be banished from our country? To be cast out from our churches and altars? For lo, certain thousands of people were taken up, children from their parents, masters from their families, women from their husbands, and were dispersed abroad into diverse countries, every one as his lot was. Some among "the thirsty Africans", as the poet speaking of this matter said, "part of them into Scythia, or among the Britons inhabiting the uttermost ends of the world from us".[194] Only Octavianus Caesar in Italy alone placed 28 colonies, and in the provinces of the empire as many as pleased him. And I know not of any one thing more pernicious than that, to the Frenchmen, us, and Spaniards.'

Chapter 24

Some strange examples of cruelty and butcherly slaughters surpassing all the mischievous massacres of our time.

'But you say further that the cruelties and butcherly slaughters of this age are such as have not been heard of before. I know your meaning, and what has been lately done.[195] Yet, upon your credit, Lipsius, tell me, has not the like been among the ancients? You are ignorant if you know it not, and scarce honest if you dissemble it. The examples are so many and ready at hand that it is a business for me to make choice of them. Have you heard of the name of Sulla, that happy man? Then are you not ignorant of his infamous and tyrannous proscription, whereby he deprived one city of four thousand seven hundred citizens?[196] And lest you should think they were of the base and meanest condition, know this that 140 of them were senators. I say nothing of the manifold murders that were done by his permission or commission. So as it was not without cause that Catulus uttered these words, "With whom shall we live at last, if we killed armed men in war, and the unarmed in peace?"[197] Not long after I read that three of Sulla's scholars being Triumviri, imitating their master, banished 300 Senators and over 2,000 gentlemen of Rome.[198] O monstrous wickedness, the like of which the sun never saw nor shall see from East to West! Read Appian if you will, and there behold the variable and loathsome spectacle of some hiding in corners, some flying away, some drawing back, others plucking forwards, children and wives making lamentations round about. I wish I were dead if any man will not affirm that humanity itself was utterly extinguished in that bloody and brutish age. These things were executed upon senators and gentlemen of the best sort, even knights; that is, almost upon so many kings and princes.

But by chance have the common sort tasted not of this sauce? Yes, mark how the very same Sulla, "when four legions of the contrary party had yielded to his fidelity, he caused them every man to be put to the sword in a common village, they crying out in vain for mercy at his treacherous hands".[199] The pitiful groanings of which men at their death, coming to the senate, and the senators turning about amazed, "O reverent fathers", he said, "let this be. Only a few seditious persons are punished by my appointment". And surely I know not at which of these two I should marvel most, that a man could find in his heart to commit such a fact or to utter such words. What? Will you have yet more examples of cruelty? Hear then Servius Galba assembling together the people of three towns in Spain as if he had to treat of something of their wealth, caused suddenly to be murdered 7,000 among whom was the flower of all the youth.[200] In the same country L. Licinius Lucullus the consul, contrary to his promise made at the yielding of the Caucaeans, sent his soldiers into their city and slew of them 20,000.[201] Octavianus Augustus when he took Perusia "choosing out 300 of those that had yielded, as well of the better sort as of the vulgar, slew them in the manner of sacrifices before an altar newly erected to the Deified Julius",[202] Antonius Caracalla being (for some kind of jests I know not what) offended with them of Alexandria, entering the city in peaceable manner, and calling out all their youth into a fair field, enclosed them with his soldiers and at a sign given, killed them every man. Using the like cruelty against all residue, whereby he left utterly without an inhabitant that populous city, king Mithridates by one letter caused to be murdered eighty thousand citizens of Rome that were dispersed abroad throughout Asia about their marchandise and other affairs.[203] Volesus Messala, being proconsul of Asia, slew with the sword 300 in one day and then walking proudly among the corpses with his hands cast abroad, as though he had achieved a worthy enterprise, cried out, "Oh kingly deed!"[204] I speak only of profane and wicked heathens; but behold also among those that are in name consecrated to the true God, Theodosius the prince, most mischievously and fraudulently calling together at Thessalonica 7,000 innocent persons, as it were to see plays, sent in soldiers among them and slew them. Than which fact there is not any more impious among the impieties of the old tyrants. Go now to my countrymen of Belgica, and complain of the tyranny and treachery of princes in this age.'

Chapter 25

The tyranny of our time is extenuated. Showing that the same is a thing incident either to the nature, or malice of men. And that both external and internal oppressions have been in old time.

'Finally, you do accuse moreover the tyranny of these times, and the oppressions of body and mind. It is not my purpose ambitiously to extol this our age, or to afflict and grieve it. For what good would come of that? I will speak of that that makes for my purpose of comparison. When were these evils not rife? And where not? Name me any age without some notable tyranny, or any country? If you can do so (let me abide the danger of this hazard) I will confess that we are the most wretched of all wretches. Why do you hold your peace? I see the old taunting by-word is true, "that all good princes may be written at large in the compass of our ring". For it is naturally given to men's disposition to use imperial authority insolently, neither can they easily keep a mean in that thing which is above mediocrity. Even we ourselves that thus complain of tyranny do bear in our breasts some seed of it, and many of us do not lack will to perform it, but ability. The serpent being numbed with cold has yet his poison within him, but does not cast it out. So it is with us, whom only imbecility keeps back from doing harm, and a certain coldness of fortune. Give strength, give fit opportunity or instruments, and I fear me that they which now are so querulous against mighty men will be most unruly themselves. We have examples in the common course of our life. See how this father tyrannises over his children, that master over his servants, another schoolmaster over his scholars. Every one of these is a Phalaris in his kind.[205] And they do stir up waves as much within their rivers as kings do in their great seas. Neither are other living creatures free from this natural disposition, among whom many do exercise their cruelty upon their like in kind, both in the air, earth, and water. As it is well said of Varro:

> So little fish to great ones are a prey,
> And silly birds, the greedy hawk does slay.[206]

You reply yet that all these are only oppressions of the body. But now this passes all the rest, that we endure also servile oppressions of our minds. Is it so indeed? Of our minds? Take heed this be not spoken more enviously than truly. He seems to me to know neither himself nor the celestial nature of the mind which thinks it may be oppressed or constrained. For no outward force can ever make you will what you will not, or to believe what you believe not. A man may have power upon this bond or fetter of the mind, but not over the mind itself. A tyrant has power to loose it from the body, but not to unloose the nature of it. Such things as be pure, everlasting, and of fiery nature, set nought by all external and violent handling. But, say you, it is not lawful for me to express my mind freely. Be it so;

herein your tongue alone is bridled, not your mind. Your judgement is not restrained, but your acts. But this is a strange course and never before heard of! Alas, good man, how are you deceived? How many could I recount to you who for their unadvised tongues have suffered punishment of all their senses under tyrants? How many of them have endeavoured to force and constrain men's judgements? Yes their judgements, I say, in matters of religion. The kings of Persia and of the East made it an ordinary custom to be adored. And we know that Alexander assumed to himself the same divine honour, his own plain countrymen the Macedonians disliking it. Among the Romans that good and moderate prince Augustus had his priests in all provinces, even in private houses, as a god. Caligula, cutting off the heads from the images of their heathen gods, caused the likeness of his own to be put in their steads; and with a ridiculous impiety he erected a temple, instituted priests and most exquisite sacrifices in honour of his own majesty. Nero would needs be taken for Apollo, and the principal citizens were by him put to death under this pretence "because they had never sacrificed before the heavenly voice".[207] As for Domitian, he was commonly called "our god" and "our lord". What vanity, Lipsius, or impiety were it to speak anything at this day against any king? I purpose not to sail nearer this gulf, in to which no stormy winds of ambition shall ever draw or drive me, "for the reward of silence is void of danger".[208] I will allege only one testimony concerning all this matter of servitude in old times, and that out of your familiar writer, which I would have you well to mark. Tacitus, writing of Domitian's time, has thus: "We read that it was made a matter of death, when Paetus Thrasea was praised to Arulenus Justicus, or Priscus Helvidius to Herennius Senecio. Neither extended this cruelty to those authors only, but also to their books, the Triumviri having the charge committed to them to see the monuments of those excellent wits burned in open view of the people, and in the marketplace. In truth they supposed by that fire utterly to abolish or suppress the speech of the people of Rome, the liberties of the Senate, and the consciences of all mankind. Expelling moreover all professors of wisdom, and banishing all good arts, to the intent that no honest thing should remain in use. Surely we have given a notable experiment of patience; and as the old ages have seen the very highest degree in liberty, so have we felt the uttermost extremity in servitude. The very society of speaking and hearing being taken from us by straight inquisitions. We should also have lost our memory with our voice, if so be it lay in our power to forget, as it does to hold our peace.'"[209]

Chapter 26

Finally, it is proved that these evils are neither strange nor new; but at all times common to all people and nations. And in this some comfort is sought for.

'Neither will I add any more touching comparison, I come now to the last troop of my legion which fights against novelty, but briefly, and with contempt of it. For it shall rather gather up the spoils of the conquered enemies than be forced to any fierce grappling with them. For in very truth, what is there here that can be accounted new to any man unless that you yourself being new born are a novice in human affairs? Well spoke Crantor and wisely, who had ever this verse in his mouth, "Woe is me, what woe is me? We have suffered but things pertaining to men".[210] For these miseries do but wheel about continually, and circularly run about this circle of the world. Why do you sigh for the happening of these heavy accidents? Why do you marvel at them?

> O Agamemnon, Atreus your sire
> Begat you not to joyfulness alone.
> As mirth, so sorrow sometimes is your hire;
> Mortal you are, and to this were you borne.
> Yet though you strive, and stubbornly refuse,
> God having willed it so, you cannot choose.[211]

This rather is a thing to be wondered at, if any man were lawlessly exempted from this common law, and carried none of that burden of which every man bears a part. Solon, seeing a very friend of his at Athens mourning piteously, brought him into a high tower and showed him underneath all the houses in that great city, saying to him 'Think with yourself how many sundry mournings in times past have been in all these houses, how many at this present are, and in time to come shall be; and leave off to bewail the miseries of mortal folk, as if they were your own".[212] I would wish you, Lipsius, to do the like in this wide world. But because you cannot in deed and fact go to, do it a little while in conceit and imagination. Suppose, if it please you, that you are with me on the top of that high hill Olympus; behold from there all towns, provinces, and kingdoms of the world, and think that you see even so many enclosures full of human calamities. These are but only theatres and places for the purpose prepared, in which Fortune plays her bloody tragedies. Neither cast your eyes far hence. Do you see Italy? It is not yet full thirty years ago since it had rest from cruel and sharp wars on every side. Do you behold the large country of Germany? There were lately in her great sparks of civil dissension, which do begin to burn again, and unless I am deceived will grow to a more consuming flame. Britain? In it there have been continual wars and slaughters, and in that now it rests awhile in peace, must be referred to the government of a peaceable sex.[213] What of France? See and pity her. Even now a festered gangrene of bloody war creeps through her every joint. So it is in all the world besides. Which things think well upon, Lipsius, and by this communication or participation of miseries, lighten your own. And like they which rode gloriously in triumph, had a servant behind their backs who in the midst of all their triumphant jollity cried out often times "you are a man", so let this be ever as a prompter by your side, that these things are human, or appertaining to men. For as labour being divided between many is easy, even so likewise is sorrow.'

Chapter 27

The Conclusion of the whole conference, with a short admonition to the often repeating and careful consideration thereof.

'I have displayed all my forces, Lipsius, and all my arguments. You have heard as much as I thought necessary to be spoken on the behalf of Constancy against Sorrow. Which God grant it be not only pleasing but profitable to you, and that it do not so much delight as benefit or help you. As certainly it will do if it sinks not into your ears alone, but also into your mind. And if, having once heard the same, you suffer it not to lie still and wither away as feed scattered upon the face of the earth. Finally, if you repeat the same often, and take due consideration of it. Because that as fire is not forced out of the flint with one stroke, so in these frozen hearts of ours, the lurking and languishing sparks of honesty are not kindled with the first stroke of admonition. Which, that they may at the last be thoroughly enkindled in you, not in words or appearance, but in deed and fact, I humbly and reverently seek that eternal and celestial fire.'

When he had thus spoken, he rose up hastily, and said 'I am going, Lipsius, for this south sun is to me a token of dinner time. Follow after me.' 'Even so', said I, 'gladly and with a very good will. And now may I rightly sing together with you in the antiphony, as is used in holy ceremonies,

I have escaped the evil, and found the good.[214]

NOTES TO TRANSLATION

1. This prefatory text is entitled *Ad Lectorem, de consilio meo scriptionis et fine*, and was not translated by Stradling. This English version is based upon that of Nathaniel Wanley (1670), as printed in Kirk, 205-08. It is not included in Neumann's edition; where necessary I have consulted the Latin text in Du Bois and in *Opera* 4,517-19. The paragraph breaks are mine.

2. Lucretius, *De Rerum Natura* 2.8.

3. *gên pro gês*; see Aeschylus, *Prometheus Vinctus* 682.

4. See Cicero, *Ad Familiares* 7.30.1 (= 265.1 Shackleton Bailey); the reference is to a family infamous for incest and murder.

5. Aristophanes, *Lysistrata* 772.

6. *Adfectus*; this is Lipsius' Latin equivalent for *pathê*, often translated as 'passions' or 'emotions'.

7. Homer, *Iliad* 14.130.

8. Diogenes the Cynic, reported in Diogenes Laertius 6.24 (= *SSR* V B 303).

9. Seneca, *De Tranquillitate Animi* 2.12-13.

10. Virgil, *Aeneid* 4.70-73.

11. Virgil, *Aeneid* 4.73.

12. See Horace, *Carmina* 3.1.40.

13. See Seneca, *Epistulae* 28.2; 104.7 (= *SSR* I C 535). This maxim was also taken up by Lipsius' contemporary Michel de Montaigne, *Essais* 1.39 (Thibaudet and Rat, 234; Frame, 213).

14. Virgil, *Aeneid* 3.282-83.

15. This is an allusion to the fate of Prometheus; see Hesiod, *Theogony* 521-31.

16. *Constantiam hic appello, rectum et immotum animi robur, non elati externis aut fortuitis, non depressi.*

17. *At Constantiae vera mater, Patientia & demissio animi est. Quam definio rerum quaecumque homini aliunde accident aut incidunt voluntariam & sine querela perpessionem.*

18. This image of 'dyeing' the mind can be found in both Seneca (*Epistulae* 71.31) and Marcus Aurelius (3.4, 5.16).

19. Seneca, *Epistulae* 66.12.

20. On Theseus, who used a thread to find his way through the Minotaur's labyrinth, see Plutarch's *Life of Theseus*.

21. Seneca, *Epistulae* 73.16; see also 41.2.

22. i.e. false goods.

23. i.e. false evils.

24. *Cupiditas & Gaudium; Metus & Dolor*. This echoes the Stoic analysis of emotions recounted by Cicero, *Tusculanae Disputationes* 3.24-25 (= *SVF* 3.385), 4.11-14. There, the four types listed are lust (*libido*) and delight (*laetitia*), fear (*metus*) and distress (*aegritudo*).

25. Afranius, quoted in Cicero, *Tusculanae Disputationes* 4.45.

26. Ennius, quoted in Cicero, *Tusculanae Disputationes* 2.38.

27. Ennius, quoted in Cicero, *Tusculanae Disputationes* 3.44.

28. *Simulatio, Pietas, Miseratio.*

29. Ennius, *Annales* 338 (Skutsch).

30. See Aulus Gellius, *Noctes Atticae* 6.5.

31. Cicero, *Tusculanae Disputationes* 5.108 (= *SSR* I C 492); see also Plutarch, *De Exilio* 600f; Musonius Rufus, *Reliquiae* 9 (42,1-2 Hense).

32. Horace, *Satirae* 2.3.72.

33. Pindar, *Nemea* 1.53-54.

34. Euripides, *Alcestis* 1047-48.

35. i.e. Musonius Rufus. In fact, the line in question is by Epictetus, and is from *Dissertationes* 3.23.30. Epictetus quotes Musonius immediately beforehand, and this no doubt led to Lipsius' confusion here.

36. Euripides, *Phoenissae* 358-59.

37. i.e. Lucius Antonius, younger brother of Marcus Antonius, and known as 'Pietas'.

38. Horace, *Carmina* 3.2.13.

39. See Plato, *Phaedrus* 270a (= DK 59A15); Diogenes Laertius 2.7 (= DK 59A1). On Anaxagoras see *DPhA* 1,183-87.

40. Here Lipsius summarises the four arguments that form the heart of *De Constantia* and occupy most of the remainder of the text. The first is dealt with in 1.14, the second in 1.15-22, the third (after an interlude) in 2.6-17, and the fourth in 2.18-26.

41. Ps.-Aristotle, *De Mundo* 6, 400b6-11.

42. Virgil, *Georgica* 4.221-22.

43. Pindar, *Olympia* 14.9-10.

44. See Homer, *Iliad* 8.19-20.

45. Euripides, *Orestes* 2.

46. See Horace, *Carmina* 3.4.42.

47. Here Lipsius echoes the famous Stoic dog-cart analogy, reported by

Hippolytus, *Refutatio* 1.21 (= *SVF* 2.975), and also a text attributed to Cleanthes by Epictetus (*Enchiridion* 53) and Seneca (*Epistulae* 107.10; both *SVF* 1.527). For further discussion see Bobzien (1998), 345-57.

48. Seneca, *De Vita Beata* 15.7.

49. See Diogenes Laertius 1.35 (= DK 11A1).

50. Plato, *Leges* 741a.

51. *krisis bebaia kai ametatreptos dunamis têr pronoias*; from the teachings of Hermes Trismegistus to Ammon, in Stobaeus 1.4.7b (1,72,4-5 Wachsmuth-Hense), which is printed as Stobaeus Excerpt 13 in Scott, *Hermetica* 1,434. For Hermes see n. 64 below.

52. Sophocles, *Oedipus Coloneus* 607-09.

53. i.e. 1572.

54. Augustine, *De Civitate Dei* 21.8 (*CCSL* 48,771).

55. i.e. Attila the Hun.

56. i.e. Rome.

57. For Anaxarchus, who followed Alexander the Great on his campaigns, see DK 72 and *DPhA* 1,188-91.

58. Pindar, *Pythia* 8.95-96.

59. *hêsuchô podi.*

60. i.e. the three fates.

61. See Plautus, *Miles Gloriosus* 17-18.

62. Homer, *Odyssey* 3.147.

63. Of these four kinds of destiny (or fate), the first (mathematical) is Chaldaean, the second (natural) is Aristotelian, the third (violent) is Stoic, and the fourth (true) is Lipsius' own, explicated in 1.19.

64. From the teachings of Hermes Trismegistus to Ammon, in Stobaeus 1.5.20 (1,82,3-10 Wachsmuth-Hense), and printed in Scott, *Hermetica* 1,434. Mercurius, the god of traders, is the Roman equivalent of the Greek Hermes. Lipsius uses this Latin equivalent for 'Hermes' to refer to Hermes Trismegistus, whose name is a translation of the Egyptian 'Thoth the Very Great'. For further information see *DPhA* 3,641-50.

65. See Alexander of Aphrodisias, *De Fato* 6 (169,18-171,17 Bruns). For the full text and a translation see Sharples (1983).

66. Theophrastus *apud* Stobaeus 1.6.17c (1,89,3-4 Wachsmuth-Hense), and printed as Theophrastus fr. 503 in W.W. Fortenbaugh, P.M. Huby, R.W. Sharples, D. Gutas, eds, *Theophrastus of Eresus* (Leiden: Brill, 1992).

67. i.e. the *De Mundo*, now thought to be spurious.

68. *tên heimarmenên ouk aitian mê, tropon de tina aitias sumbebêkota pôs tois tês anankês tetragmenois.* This presumably derives from one of the Greek Aristotelian commentators; Neumann has not been able to identify its source, and nor have I.

69. Seneca, *Naturales Quaestiones* 2.36.
70. Chrysippus *apud* Stobaeus 1.5.15 (1,79,1-2 Wachsmuth-Hense = *SVF* 2.913).
71. Seneca, *De Providentia* 5.8.
72. See Aulus Gellius, *Noctes Atticae* 7.2.1-11 (= *SVF* 2.1000).
73. Zeno *apud* Aetius, *Placita* 1.27.5 (322b10-11 Diels = *SVF* 1.176).
74. *logon aidion tês pronoias.* I have been unable to trace this text. Neither Lagrée nor Neumann has managed to locate it either. One possible source is Aetius, *Placita* 1.28.2-3 (323a7-16 Diels).
75. *theon apophaiteto tên heimarmenên.* I have been unable to trace this text. Neither Lagrée nor Neumann has managed to locate it either.
76. Seneca, *De Beneficiis* 4.7.1-2.
77. i.e. Aristotle, writing to Alexander the Great.
78. Ps.-Aristotle, *De Mundo* 7, 401b8-10.
79. *tas en haidou triakadas.*
80. On this see Varro, *De Lingua Latina* 6.52.
81. *pendentem a divino consilio seriem ordinemque caussarum,* from Giovanni Pico della Mirandola, *Disputationum in Astrologiam* 4.4 (*Opera Omnia* 1,530). Giovanni Pico della Mirandola (1463-94), Italian philosopher and humanist, published this work in 1496. See Schmitt *et al.* (1988), 832.
82. *kegchron trupan,* see Galen, *De Praenotione ad Posthumum* 14,605 (Kühn).
83. See e.g. Augustine, *De Civitate Dei* 5.8-11 (*CCSL* 47,135-42), where Augustine discusses fate, providence, and necessity.
84. See Suetonius, *Domitianus* 16.1-2.
85. Homer, *Iliad* 16.426-38; i.e. free him from his bonds.
86. i.e. rotates around.
87. In his *De Divinatione.*
88. Augustine, *De Civitate Dei* 5.9 (*CCSL* 47,137). This whole chapter (along with 5.8 and 5.10-11) was probably an important text for Lipsius, for in it Augustine comments on Cicero's treatment of the Stoic doctrine of fate, and so offers an authoritative example of how a Christian should approach the topic.
89. This reference to Damascene is in the first edition of the Latin text, but it is not in the more recent editions by Du Bois and Neumann.
90. See Euclides in *SSR* II A 17. On Euclides see *DPhA* 3,272-77.
91. *peri theôn lege hôs eisin,* see Diogenes Laertius 1.88.
92. A reference to Archimedes; see Cicero, *De Finibus* 5.50.
93. Virgil, *Aeneid* 6.376.
94. Epictetus, *Enchiridion* 19.
95. Euripides, *Bacchae* 794-95.
96. This is a version of the famous 'lazy argument' (*argos logos*), for which

see Cicero, *De Fato* 28-29. For discussion see Bobzien (1998), 182-98.

97. *media & auxiliante caussa.*

98. This echoes Chrysippus' response to the 'lazy argument', for which see Cicero, *De Fato* 30 (= *SVF* 2.956), with discussion in Bobzien (1998), 199-233.

99. Vellius Paterculus, *Historia Romana* 2.57.3.

100. Vellius Paterculus, *Historia Romana* 2.118.4.

101. *mê theomacheîn*; see Euripides, *Iphigenie in Aulis* 1408.

102. Diogenes Laertius 1.50; see also Plutarch, *Solon* 30.

103. See Livy, *Ab Urbe Condita* 22.49-61.

104. Diogenes Laertius 6.93 (= *SSR* V H 31).

105. Homer, *Iliad* 24.522-24.

106. See Apollodorus, *Bibliotheca* 1.9.28.

107. *theôn trophên.*

108. Ennius, *Annales* 163.

109. This is a reference is to 'Hortensius who (it is said) wore mourning apparel for the loss of a lamprey'. See Pliny, *Naturalis Historia* 9.171-72.

110. Homer, *Odyssey* 7.119.

111. Scipio Africanus, in Cicero, *De Officiis* 3.1.

112. Horace, *Carmina* 1.26.3-4.

113. i.e. the Muses.

114. Augustine, *De Ordine* 1.2.4 (*CCSL* 29,91).

115. See Homer's *Odyssey*, Book 18.

116. Menander, *Sententiae Singulares* 865 (Jaekel).

117. See Athenaeus, *Deipnosophistae* 159c.

118. Lipsius himself did publish an edition of the works of Tactitus in 1574, ten years before publishing *De Constantia.*

119. See Ovid, *Metamorphoses* 12.171-209.

120. i.e. Wisdom.

121. See 1.14 and 1.15-22 above.

122. Aulus Gellius, *Noctes Atticae* 5.12.4.

123. Plato, *Respublica* 379b.

124. Seneca, *Epistulae* 95.48-50.

125. Augustine, *Enchiridion* 8.27 (*CCSL* 46,64).

126. Boethius, *Philosophiae Consolationis* 4.Pr.6.185-86.

127. i.e. Vespasian and Titus.

128. Homer, *Odyssey* 5.90.

129. Demetrius the Cynic, in Seneca, *De Providentia* 3.3. For Dementrius see *DPhA* 2,622-23.

130. See Cicero, *Paradoxa Stoicorum* 8; Valerius Maximus, *Facta et Dicta*

Memorabilia 7.2.ext.3. This phrase is also attributed to Stilpo; see e.g. Seneca, *De Constantia Sapientis* 5.6; Diogenes Laertius 2.115 (both *SSR* II O 15).

131. Marcus Atilius Regulus, on whom see Cicero, *De Officiis* 3.99-100.

132. Roman jurist, murdered by the Emperor Caracalla.

133. Philemon fr. 246 (*CAF* 2,539).

134. Virgil, *Aeneid* 6.620.

135. Lucretius, *De Rerum Natura* 6.72.

136. *kolasis, all' ou timôria*, see Aristotle, *Ars Rhetorica* 1.10, 1369b13.

137. Boethius, *Philosophiae Consolationis* 4.Pr.4.42-44.

138. Wisd. 11.20.

139. Seneca, *Epistulae* 74.20.

140. Lucretius, *De Rerum Natura* 2.1103-04.

141. Salvianus, *De Gubernatione Dei* 1.6 (*PL* 53,38d).

142. Tacitus, *Annales* 1.6.

143. Sophocles fr. 919.

144. Synesius, *De Providentia* 2.5 (*PG* 66,1273b).

145. Euripides *apud* Plutarch, *De Sera Numinis Vindicta* 549a

146. *akolouos tês adikias hê timôria*, see Plato, *Leges* 728c.

147. *hêlikiôtis*; neither I nor Neumann have been able to trace this in Hesiod.

148. Tacitus, *Annales* 6.6.

149. i.e. Dionysius.

150. Horace, *Carmina* 3.1.17-18.

151. Tacitus, *Annales* 6.6.

152. Nero, in Suetonius, *Nero* 47.3.

153. In the first edition of 1584, this section is simply a continuation of ch. 14, with subsequent chapters numbered one less than they are here. The third edition of 1586 already has this new division, with Book 2 having 27 chapters rather than the original 26. I have been unable to consult the second edition of 1585 to determine precisely when this new division was added to the text.

154. See Cicero, *Tusculanae Disputationes* 3.27, who reports that after his expulsion from Syracuse, Dionysius became a schoolmaster in Corinth.

155. Plutarch, *Cato Minor* 53.2.

156. Plutarch, *Brutus* 51.1.

157. Pliny, *Naturalis Historia* 7.150.

158. Horace, *Carmina* 3.2.31-32.

159. See Juvenal, *Saturae* 13.78.

160. Diogenes Laertius 1.36 (= DK 11A1).

161. Source unknown.

162. Horace, *Carmina* 3.6.1-2.
163. Plautus, *Captivi* 313.
164. Hesiod, *Opera et Dies* 240-43.
165. See 2 Sam. 24.15
166. See Tacitus, *Annales* 14.44.
167. Augustine, *De Civitate Dei* 18.18 (*CCSL* 48,608).
168. i.e. Castor and Pollux.
169. See Pliny, *Naturalis Historia* 24.43, which has Democrates rather than Demochares as the name of the physician.
170. e.g. Socrates, Cato the Younger, and Seneca.
171. See Epictetus, *Dissertationes* 2.16.22.
172. *mormolukeia*; see e.g. Plato, *Phaedo* 77e; Epictetus, *Dissertationes* 2.1.15.
173. Amphis fr. 15 (*CAF* 2,240).
174. Cicero, *Tusculanae Disputationes* 2.20, quoting his Latin version of Sophocles, *Trachiniae* 1046.
175. *eschatôn eschaton*.
176. Euripides, *Hippolytus* 822-23.
177. Neumann has 700, Stradling 1700. The 1584 edition has *mille* DCC.
178. Neumann has 100,000, Stradling 1,000,000. The 1584 edition has *decies centena millia*.
179. This is Neumann's total; Stradling has 124,000, which doesn't tally with the other figures that Stradling himself prints.
180. See Plutarch, *De Defectu Oraculorum* 414a.
181. See Augustine, *De Civitate Dei*, and Orosius, *Historiarum*.
182. Pliny, *Naturalis Historia* 7.92.
183. i.e. Pompeius Magnus.
184. See Plutarch, *Cato Maior* 10.3.
185. i.e. America.
186. *gurgulinculos minutos*, i.e. *curculiunculus minutos*. Neither I nor Neumann have been able to identify the comic poet in question.
187. See 2 Sam. 24.15.
188. See Zonaras, *Annales* 12.21 (*PG* 134,1061b).
189. See Procopius, *De Bellis* 2.23.1-2.
190. See Orosius, *Historiarum* 5.11 (*PL* 31,942a).
191. Zonaras, *Annales* 18.17 (*PG* 135,284b).
192. See Zosimus, *Historia Nova* 6.11.
193. See Procopius, *De Bellis* 6.20.27-29.
194. Virgil, *Eclogae* 1.65-66.
195. Stradling comments in the margin 'I take it he means the Massacre at Paris on St Bartholomew's Day', in 1572, on which see Briggs (1998), 19-23.

196. See Valerius Maximus, *Facta et Dicta Memorabilia* 9.2.1.

197. Catulus, in Orosius, *Historiarum* 5.21 (*PL* 31,972b).

198. See Appian, *Bellum Civile* 4.2.5, but Appian says to be killed, not banished.

199. Valerius Maximus, *Facta et Dicta Memorabilia* 9.2.1.

200. Valerius Maximus, *Facta et Dicta Memorabilia* 9.6.2, who has 8,000, not 7,000.

201. See Appian, *Bellum Hispanicum* 9.52.

202. Suetonius, *Augustus* 15.

203. See Valerius Maximus, *Facta et Dicta Memorabilia* 9.2.ext.3.

204. See Seneca, *De Ira* 2.5.5. Lipsius cites this in Greek (*ô pragma basilikon*); Seneca has the same phrase, although only in Latin (*o rem regiam*).

205. i.e. a cruel tyrant. Pharalis was a notorious tyrant; see e.g. Seneca, *De Ira* 2.5.1.

206. Varro, *Saturarum Menippearum Fragmenta* 289.

207. See Tacitus, *Annales* 16.22.

208. Simonides *apud* Plutarch, *Regum et Imperatorum Apophthegmata* 207d.

209. Tacitus, *Agricola* 2.

210. Diogenes Laertius, 4.26; on Crantor see *DPhA* 2,482-84.

211. Euripides, *Iphigenia in Aulis* 29-34.

212. See Valerius Maximus, *Facta et Dicta Memorabilia* 7.2.ext.2.

213. Presumably a reference to Queen Elizabeth I.

214. Demosthenes, *De Corona* 259.

BIBLIOGRAPHY

This bibliography is restricted to items that I have consulted and have found to be of use. It does not pretend to be a complete bibliography of work on Lipsius. Editions of ancient authors are not included.

Anderton, B. (1922a), 'A Stoic in His Garden', in his *Sketches from a Library Window* (Cambridge: Heffer), 1-9
———— (1922b), 'A Stoic of Louvain: Justus Lipsius', in his *Sketches from a Library Window* (Cambridge: Heffer), 10-30
Barbour, R. (1998), *English Epicures and Stoics: Ancient Legacies in Early Stuart Culture* (Amherst: University of Massachusetts Press)
Bayle, P. (1991), *Historical and Critical Dictionary: Selections*, trans. R.H. Popkin (Indianapolis: Hackett)
Blom, H.W., and L.C. Winkel (2004), eds, *Grotius and the Stoa* (Assen: Royal Van Gorcum)
Bobzien, S. (1998), *Determinism and Freedom in Stoic Philosophy* (Oxford: Clarendon Press)
Boter, G. (1999), *The Encheiridion of Epictetus and its Three Christian Adaptations* (Leiden: Brill)
Bouwsma, W.J. (1975), 'The Two Faces of Humanism: Stoicism and Augustinianism in Renaissance Thought', in H.A. Oberman and T.A. Brady, eds, *Itinerarium Italicum: The Profile of the Italian Renaissance in the Mirror of its European Transformations* (Leiden: Brill), 3-60
Briggs, R. (1998), *Early Modern France: 1560-1715* (Oxford: Oxford University Press)
Brooke, C. (2004), 'Stoicism and anti-Stoicism in the Seventeenth Century', in Blom and Winkel (2004), 93-115
Buddeus, J.F. (1724), *Analecta Historiae Philosophicae*, Editio II (Halae Saxonum)
———— (1737), *De Atheismo et Superstitione* (Traiecti ad Rehum)

Chappell, V. (1999), ed., *Hobbes and Bramhall on Liberty and Necessity* (Cambridge: Cambridge University Press)

Charron, P. (1601), *De la sagesse livres trois* (Bordeaux)

———— (1697), *Of Wisdom, Three Books*, trans. George Stanhope, 2 vols (London)

———— (1986), *De la sagesse*, ed. B. de Negroni (Paris: Fayard)

Clair, C. (1960), *Christopher Plantin* (London: Cassell & Company)

Colish, M.L. (1990), *The Stoic Tradition from Antiquity to the Early Middle Ages*, 2 vols (Leiden: Brill; rev. edn)

Cooper, J.M. (2004), 'Justus Lipsius and the Revival of Stoicism in Late Sixteenth Century Europe', in N. Bender and L. Krasnoff, eds, *New Essays on the History of Autonomy* (Cambridge: Cambridge University Press), 7-29

Copenhaver, B.P., and C.B. Schmitt (1992), *Renaissance Philosophy* (Oxford: Oxford University Press)

DeBrabander, F. (2004), 'Psychotherapy and Moral Perfection: Spinoza and the Stoics on the Prospect of Happiness', in Strange and Zupko (2004), 198-213

Deitz, L., and A. Wiehe-Deitz (1997), 'Francisco de Quevedo', in Kraye (1997a), 210-25

Diderot, D. (1751-65), ed., *Encyclopédie, ou Dictionnaire Raisonné des Sciences, des Arts et des Métiers* (Neufchastel)

Du Vair, G. (1622), *A Buckler Against Adversitie or A Treatise of Constance*, trans. Andrew Court (London)

———— (1945), *De la sainte philosophie, Philosophie morale des Stoïques*, ed. G. Michaut (Paris: Vrin)

———— (1951), *The Moral Philosophie of the Stoicks*, trans. Thomas James, ed. Rudolf Kirk (New Brunswick: Rutgers University Press)

Ebbesen, S. (2004), 'Where Were the Stoics in the Late Middle Ages?', in Strange and Zupko (2004), 108-31

Enfield, W. (1819), *The History of Philosophy, From the Earliest Times to the Beginning of the Present Century, Drawn up from Brucker's Historia Critica Philosophiae*, 2 vols (London)

Ettinghausen, H. (1972), *Francisco de Quevedo and the Neostoic Movement* (Oxford: Oxford University Press)

Eymard d'Angers, J. (1976), *Recherches sur le Stoicisme aux XVIe et XVIIe siècles* (Hildesheim: Georg Olms)

Gerlo, A. (1988), ed., *Juste Lipse (1547-1606)*, Travaux de l'Institut Inter-universitaire pour l'étude de la Renaissance et de l'Humanisme 9 (Brussels: University Press)

Gerlo, A., *et al.* (1978-), eds, *Iusti Lipsi Epistolae*, 13 vols to date (Brussels: Paleis der Academiëu)

Holyoake, J. (1983), *Montaigne, Essais* (London: Grant & Cutler)

Inwood, B. (2003), ed., *The Cambridge Companion to The Stoics* (Cambridge: Cambridge University Press)

James, S. (1993), 'Spinoza the Stoic', in T. Sorell, ed., *The Rise of Modern Philosophy* (Oxford: Clarendon Press), 289-316

Kraye, J. (1997a), ed., *Cambridge Translations of Renaissance Philosophical Texts, Volume 1: Moral Philosophy* (Cambridge: Cambridge University Press)

————— (1997b), 'Angelo Poliziano', in Kraye (1997a), 192-99

————— (2004), 'Stoicism in the Renaissance from Petrarch to Lipsius', in Blom and Winkel (2004), 21-45

Kraye, J., and M.W.F. Stone (2000), eds, *Humanism and Early Modern Philosophy* (London: Routledge)

Kristeller, P.O. (1984), 'Stoic and Neoplatonic Sources of Spinoza's *Ethics*', *History of European Ideas* 5, 1-15

Lagrée, J. (1994), *Juste Lipse et la restauration du stoïcisme: Étude et traduction des traités stoïciens De la constance, Manuel de philosophie stoïcienne, Physique des stoïciens* (Paris: Vrin)

————— (1999a), 'Juste Lipse: destins et Providence', in Moreau (1999a), 77-93

————— (1999b), 'La vertu stoïcienne de constance', in Moreau (1999a), 94-116

————— (2004), 'Constancy and Coherence', in Strange and Zupko (2004), 148-76

Lapidge, M. (1988), 'The Stoic Inheritance', in P. Dronke, ed., *A History of Twelfth-Century Western Philosophy* (Cambridge: Cambridge University Press), 81-112

Laureys, M. (1998), ed., *The World of Justus Lipsius: A Contribution Towards his Intellectual Biography*, Bulletin de l'Institut Historique Belge de Rome 68 (Brussels & Rome: Brepols)

Levi, A.H.T. (2000), 'The Relationship of Stoicism and Scepticism: Justus Lipsius', in Kraye and Stone (2000), 91-106

Long, A.A. (2003), 'Stoicism in the Philosophical Tradition: Spinoza,

Lipsius, Butler', in Inwood (2003), 365-92

Marenbon, J., and G. Orlandi (2001), *Peter Abelard, Collationes* (Oxford: Clarendon Press)

Marin, M. (1988), 'L'influence de Sénèque sur Juste Lipse', in Gerlo (1988), 119-26

Matheron, A. (1999), 'Le moment stoicien de l'*Éthique* de Spinoza', in Moreau (1999a), 302-16

McCrea, A. (1997), *Constant Minds: Political Virtue and the Lipsian Paradigm in England, 1584-1650* (Toronto: University of Toronto Press)

Méchoulan, H. (1999), 'Quevedo stoïcien?', in Moreau (1999a), 189-203

Monsarrat, G.D. (1984), *Light from the Porch: Stoicism and English Renaissance Literature* (Paris: Didier-Erudition)

Montaigne, M. de (1962), *Oeuvres complètes*, ed. A. Thibaudet and M. Rat, Bibliothèque de la Pléiade (Paris: Gallimard)

———— (2003), *The Complete Works: Essays, Travel Journal, Letters*, trans. D.M. Frame (London: Everyman's Library)

Moreau, P.-F. (1999a), ed., *Le stoïcisme au XVIe et au XVIIe siècle* (Paris: Albin Michel)

———— (1999b), 'Calvin: fascination et critique du stoïcisme', in Moreau (1999a), 51-64

Morford, M. (1991), *Stoics and Neostoics: Rubens and the Circle of Lipsius* (Princeton: Princeton University Press)

———— (1998), 'Towards an Intellectual Biography of Justus Lipsius – Pieter Paul Rubens', in Laureys (1998), 387-403

Moss, A. (1998), 'The *Politica* of Justus Lipsius and the Commonplace-Book', *Journal of the History of Ideas* 59, 421-36

Normore, C. (2004), 'Abelard's Stoicism and Its Consequences', in Strange and Zupko (2004), 132-47

Oestreich, G. (1982), *Neostoicism and the Early Modern State*, trans. D. McLintock (Cambridge: Cambridge University Press)

Oliver, R.P. (1954), *Niccolo Perotti's Version of The Enchiridion of Epictetus* (Urbana: University of Illinois Press)

Osler, M.J. (1991), ed., *Atoms, Pneuma, and Tranquillity: Epicurean and Stoic Themes in European Thought* (Cambridge: Cambridge University Press)

Panizza, L.A. (1991), 'Stoic Psychotherapy in the Middle Ages and

Renaissance: Petrarch's *De Remediis*', in Osler (1991), 39-65

Papy, J. (2004), 'Lipsius' (Neo-)Stoicism: Constancy between Christian Faith and Stoic Virtue', in Blom and Winkel (2004), 47-71

Pascal, B. (1995), *Pensées and Other Writings*, trans. H. Levi (Oxford: Oxford University Press)

Pico della Mirandola, G. (1557-73), *Opera Omnia*, 2 vols (Basel; facs. repr. Hildesheim: Georg Olms, 1969)

Popkin, R.H. (1979), *The History of Scepticism from Erasmus to Spinoza* (Berkeley: University of California Press)

Prinz, W. (1973), 'The *Four Philosophers* by Rubens and the Pseudo-Seneca in Seventeenth-Century Painting', *Art Bulletin* 55, 410-28

Rawski, C.H. (1991), *Petrarch, Remedies for Fortune Fair and Foul*, 5 vols (Bloomington: Indiana University Press)

Reynolds, L.D. (1965), *The Medieval Tradition of Seneca's Letters* (Oxford: Oxford University Press)

Ross, G.M. (1974), 'Seneca's Philosophical Influence', in C.D.N. Costa, ed., *Seneca* (London: Routledge & Kegan Paul), 116-65

Sandbach, F.H. (1975), *The Stoics* (London: Chatto & Windus; 2nd edn Bristol Classical Press, 1989)

Saunders, J.L. (1955), *Justus Lipsius: The Philosophy of Renaissance Stoicism* (New York: The Liberal Arts Press)

Schmitt, C.B., *et al.* (1988), eds, *The Cambridge History of Renaissance Philosophy* (Cambridge: Cambridge University Press)

Schneewind, J.B. (1998), *The Invention of Autonomy: A History of Modern Moral Philosophy* (Cambridge: Cambridge University Press)

———— (2003), *Moral Philosophy from Montaigne to Kant* (Cambridge: Cambridge University Press)

Scott, W. (1924-26), *Hermetica*, 3 vols (Oxford: Clarendon Press)

Sellars, J. (2006), *Stoicism* (Chesham: Acumen and Berkeley: University of California Press)

Senellart, M. (1999), 'Le stoïcisme dans la constitution de la pensée politique: Les *Politiques* de Juste Lipse (1589)', in Moreau (1999a), 117-39

Sharples, R.W. (1983), *Alexander of Aphrodisias on Fate: Text, Translation, and Commentary* (London: Duckworth)

Shifflett, A. (1998), *Stoicism, Politics, and Literature in the Age of Milton: War and Peace Reconciled* (Cambridge: Cambridge University Press)

Spanneut, M. (1957), *Le Stoïcisme des Pères de l'Église: De Clément de Rome à Clément d'Alexandrie* (Paris: Seuil)

———— (1973), *Permanence du Stoïcisme: De Zénon à Malraux* (Gembloux: Duculot)

Strange, S.K., and J. Zupko (2004), eds, *Stoicism: Traditions and Transformations* (Cambridge: Cambridge University Press)

Van De Bilt, A.M. (1946), *Lipsius' De Constantia en Seneca* (Nijmegen: Dekker & Van De Vegt)

Van Der Haeghen, F. (1886), *Bibliographie Lipsienne: Oeuvres de Juste Lipse*, 2 vols (Ghent/Gand: Université de Gand)

Verbeke, G. (1983), *The Presence of Stoicism in Medieval Thought* (Washington: The Catholic University of America Press)

Vico, G. (1984), *The New Science of Giambattista Vico*, trans. T.G. Bergin and M.H. Fisch (Ithaca: Cornell University Press)

Vlieghe, H. (1987), *Rubens Portraits of Identified Sitters Painted in Antwerp*, Corpus Rubenianum Ludwig Burchard 19.2 (London: Harvey Miller)

Young, R.V. (1997), 'Justus Lipsius', in Kraye (1997a), 200-9

Zanchius, J. (1930), *The Doctrine of Absolute Predestination* (London: The Sovereign Grace Union)

Zanta, L. (1914), *La renaissance du stoïcisme au XVIe siècle* (Paris: Champion)

INDEX OF PASSAGES

I include all ancient texts cited in the Introduction and the notes to the text, not just those quoted by Lipsius. Where they exist I have used the readily available Loeb Classical Library editions.

INDEX OF SUBJECTS AND NAMES

Historical examples have been omitted. See the Index of Passages for references to authors quoted by Lipsius.

151